A.S.A.P

A Street Activist's Perspective

By

Deric Muhammad

ISBN:0578140594
ISBN-13:978-0578-14059-9
Published by The Logos Publishing

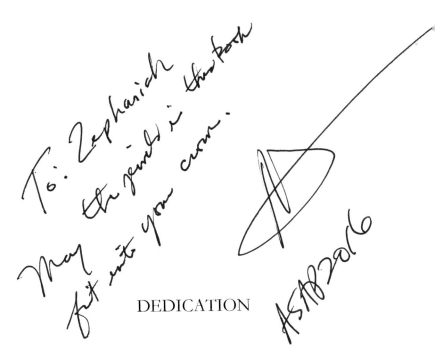

DEDICATION

To My God who created me, His messenger who
awakened me, my Minister who resurrected me, my family
who stands with me and MY PEOPLE...my reason for
doing what I do.

CONTENTS

Introduction: Made in America

Introduction

MADE IN AMERICA

"Woke up this morning looking down at the dirt and not up at it. The rest is negotiable: God willing". — @DericMuhammad

I was 11 years old the first time I saw a man bleed to death. It was a day I will never forget. We were out playing in Dyersdale Village projects, infamously nicknamed "the hole", because there was only one way in and one way out. I noticed a Black man being chased by another. I assumed they were horseplaying. Then one of them fell to the sidewalk. Seconds later, a pool of blood began pouring from underneath his body. My friends and I scrambled to find help. Within minutes, the entire neighborhood had gathered around him praying, trying to stop the bleeding and encouraging him to keep his eyes open. I remember thinking that the sidewalk in "the hole" was no place for a man to take his last breath. The loss of his life changed the course of mine.

So did the night I was awakened by fighting between my mother and her then-boyfriend. It was not the first time. He'd once beaten her so severely that I could not even recognize her when I saw her. And this was after she'd healed up. It was 3am and I had to be up for school in a few hours. I banged on the door and yelled at them to "Keep it down!" He wouldn't stop so I busted through the flimsy bedroom door of the old rented house on Sundown St. Lynn, my mom's best friend, begged me to do something because this man had plans to seriously hurt my mother. I demanded he leave. He told me "stay in child's place." That was the last thing on my mind. By the way, I think I was 12 years old by this time.

I went into combat mode and started waking up my siblings. My older sister grabbed an iron, my older brother grabbed a bat (or something) and my little brother, Jesse, even grabbed a lock and chain. We may have had a dysfunctional family, but we always meant business when it came time to protect our mother. My mom's boyfriend pulled out a pistol (concealed in a cigarette case), put it to my mother's back and led her out of the house like a hostage. He slapped her best friend so hard she flew from the living room into the kitchen. Not knowing what else to do, I grabbed a t-shaped plant stand and split him over top his head with it.

I won't get into what happened afterward. Just know that by God's grace we survived.

I remember still choosing to go the school that day. I remember the long walk home with my brothers; feeling happy about him finally being out of our lives. I was wrong. When I opened the screen door that had been broken by the violence of the night before, there he was sitting on the living room sofa. He asked me "how was school?" I wanted to kill him that day. It was then that I realized that my mother had a very bad cocaine habit. He was her dealer.

Many things happen in a human being's life that shapes his or her "perspective." We perceive reality differently, because of our unique life experiences. Like the pivotal moment when my biological father, a street hustler whom I did not meet until I was 8 years old, told me that he loved me. In the very next breath he told me "Don't be like me." He died when I was 11 year old. But his words didn't.

My dad's words are still alive in my head, just like the memory of the brother who threatened one of my "little homies" when we were teen-agers. I hit him in his face for being disrespectful. Because of my influence at the time, my friends jumped him as I was leaving. The next day I learned he was in ICU; hurt very badly. I saw him on the street many years later. I can tell he hadn't been the same since that incident. Neither have I.

Maybe I should try and forget the Christmas Eve when a man showed up at my mother's front door with an AK-47 looking for me after I'd beat him so badly that MY MOTHER had to come to his defense. I imagine she didn't want me to kill him. It was all over nonsense. Bullets flew, but we all lived to see another day. Of course, I couldn't tell it all even if I wanted to. I'm just giving you a peep into that which has shaped a "Street Activist's Perspective."

Fearing I would die in the streets of Northeast Houston, I followed my older brother in the U.S. Marine Corps. Being sent to the Gulf War and being awakened by earth shaking missiles will definitely impact your perspective. Not long after came the moment I began reading the book that changed my life, "Message to the Blackman" by Elijah Muhammad. It answered so many questions and illuminated the dark path I was traveling down. There is nothing more powerful than "divine guidance."

I remember being arrested and charged with a very serious crime against the U.S. government. I refused counsel and decided to represent myself using the principles I adopted in my readings. This is not something I advise others to do. However, I won. The charges that could have landed me in prison for over a decade were dismissed. I was only 21 years old. At the time I was crazy enough to believe I won because I was so smart. Later, I would come to know that it was Allah (God) watching over his foolish child. He had work for me to do.

I had been having Saturday study sessions about Black history and stirring up the brothers and sister on the military base. The authorities commanded me stop. Instead, I increased. They gave me orders to go to war in the Sudan. I told them I would never go back to Africa with the White man's gun in my hand. They threatened me with jail. I told them I was already in jail as a Black man in America. The Marine Corps and I could only agree on one thing. It was time for me to go.

I wasn't back in Houston very long before I witnessed a brother, Jefferrey Muhammad, being arrested for selling the Nation of Islam's Final Call Newspaper on the corner of Homestead and Tidwell. This angered me so that I abandoned my vehicle in a fast-food drive-thru, crossed the street and challenged the officers. The White officer told me to "stay back." I paid him no mind. I looked at Brother Jefferrey and asked him "what do you want to do brother." I believed we could have whipped them. He was just as angry but a lot smarter. He told me to call the mosque and report it. I then became active in the Nation of Islam shortly after that. It's no coincidence that I ended up in its Ministry of Justice addressing police brutality and other injustices. Jefferrey Muhammad remains one of my closest mentors to this day.

The previous incident reminds me of the time I was called a ni#@er by a group of Harley-Davidson-riding redneck bikers. I was so livid that I dropped my family off at a nearby restaurant and tracked them down at a local bar. I walked in ALL BY MYSELF to confront them. Most of them scattered, but two of them faced off with me. When they saw me coming after them, both reached into their back pockets and pulled out badges. They were Harris County Sheriff deputies. This is why no one can tell me there aren't racist pigs in law enforcement. My perspective comes from my experience.

So much has happened since then that has changed, chiseled and impacted my perspective on life. Like the time I bumped into the same guy who showed up at my mom's house to kill me while selling the Final Call Newspaper. To my surprise, he greeted me in peace. Weeks earlier I had been chastised by the brothers of the Fruit of Islam for keeping a pistol underneath the seat of my vehicle while selling the paper. No one had told me that we were forbidden to carry weapons. The encounter with my old enemy helped to ensure me of God's oversight. As long as you are moving in God's direction you are guaranteed God's protection.

My life has been filled with highs and lows, mountains and valleys…mansions and alleys. I've buried dozens of friends and seen others mentally and spiritually resurrected from the grave of ignorance. As a youth I was invited into the crack house. As a youth minister I was invited to the White house. My life is a twisted beauty of a movie. Like they say in the streets, "it's just different."

I contend that most Black correspondents hired by media outlets don't really speak for the masses of Black people. Their perspective is based on their research, coupled with their experiences. I love to listen to brothers like Tavis Smiley, Dr. Cornel West, Marc Lamont Hill, Roland Martin and others.

They are some of the most brilliant minds among us. However, these are polished, well-spoken scholars who more than likely have not been back to "the hood" in a very long time.

When I listen to those who "the establishment" have offered a platform to speak for Black people, I hear a serious disconnect. Much of what they say does not reflect the reality faced by every-day Black folk in America.

The views expressed in this book represent the perspective of an "on the ground" activist striving to help my people through the every-day struggles we face. It addresses some of our most critical issues; particularly, those we do not like to talk about. It deals less with what White people have done to us and more with what we must do for ourselves. This work is not intended to elicit 100% agreement from every reader. It is intended to give you a view from the ground; something that is missing among Black intelligentsia. Whether you love, hate, or are indifferent about a street activist's perspective, it's important that you remember that is was MADE IN AMERICA.

CHAPTER 1

THE A.S.A.P Mentality

"The best time to plant a tree was twenty years ago. The next best time to plant it is Now!" (African Proverb)

Integration was a trick designed to destroy the sense of urgency of Black people. Being forced to live amongst our own, do business amongst our own, worship amongst our own and go to school amongst our own gave us the false belief that we were merely surviving, when we were actually building. Now, I've heard the supporters of integration, who lived through the sixties, refer to those days of segregation as "the good ole days." Once we were able to have tea and crackers with the children of our former slave masters we thought we'd hit the lottery of humanity. This illusion gave us a "do nothing" mentality. A "do-nothing" mentality creates a "have-nothing" reality.

There is something about living through a crisis that gives the human being an "A.S.A.P" mentality. They understand the importance of achieving objectives "as soon as possible." We are more inclined to, as the Nation of Islam teaches, be quick thinking, fast moving; right down to the modern times.

Joshua, the successor of Moses, led the Israelite nation across the Jordan River during a period of a crisis. The Jordan River was a dark, muddy, and murky body of water. Every step taken across the river was met with impending danger. There was no time to waste. They had the A.S.A.P. mentality which produced the A.S.A.P. energy that got them safely to the other side.

Just as The Creator dried up the Jordan River in order for Joshua and the Israelites to get closer to the Promised Land, God has always prepared a table for Black people right here in the midst of the enemies of our progress. However, we tend to lose our sense of urgency once God has delivered us through periods of crisis. We must become like Joshua and the strong soldiers who were with him. Not only did they use the ASAP mentality to cross the Jordan River, they used that energy to conquer the city of Jericho on the other side.

What is it that rocks us to sleep in our personal lives, as well as our community life? What destroys our sense of urgency? Why does God have to keep us in a perpetual state of struggle in order to create in us a sense of NOW? The "illusion of inclusion" that integration, affirmative action and having a Black president of the United States are some factors that have disproportionately affected us. At the end of the day being Black in America is still the uphill road that it was when our forefathers set the soles of their feet onto this soil in Jamestown, Virginia in 1555. It is time that we resurrect the A.S.A.P. mentality in self and community. We have to tap into the spirit of Harriet Tubman that freed a thousand slaves and use it to free ourselves from apathy, complacency and fear. TAKE IT PERSONAL!

When your mother and father conceived you, billions of sperm were released in the process. Only one made it. That one developed into the miracle that is called YOU. If the sperm that created you had a sense of urgency ; you have it too. What's taking you so long to start that business, purchase that land, marry that "good" woman or man or commit yourself to that cause? The short time you will live on this Earth amounts to nothing when you consider how long you will be dead once it's over. YOU DO NOT HAVE TIME TO WASTE! You do not have the luxury of being afraid of the mountain that stands in front of you. Prayer before war is the soldier's protocol. You are that soldier. Make your prayer, determine your destination and go to war with all obstacles in your path.

Joshua was so focused on the Promised Land on the other side of Jordan River that it minimized his fear of the danger of crossing. Harriet Tubman was so obsessed with the freedom of her people that her fear of the slave master evaporated. There is a spiritual force within you that has the power to quicken the forward pace toward your success. Stop complaining about how cold the world is. Focus on making sure it is a better place when you leave it.

Black people in America have many issues. This book addresses some of the most critical of our time. While it is meant to create meaningful dialogue, my real motive is to create in us a sense of NOW in addressing these issues. In so many ways we have become "jaded" toward our own suffering. We make mockery of our own destructive behavior. Through television shows like "Love & Hip-Hop", as well as "Scandal", we promote that which demotes the dignity of our community. This book is small in size; but so is a match. The size of a fire is never limited to the size of the match that lights the fire. In cities all across America and beyond we must come together as a people and create a "let's get it done" mentality when it comes to addressing our issues, mapping out a strategy to solve our problems and executing a plan with perfect precision. Allow no creature comforts to destroy your sense of urgency. Let us quicken the pace toward freedom by adopting the A.S.A.P. mentality.

CHAPTER 2

Motive: The Power of Sincerity

" Your motive for doing what you do is what either lessens the spirit of God or brings God into the equation with you"- Minister Louis Farrakhan

Imagine a man running into a blazing inferno to save an elderly woman. Once he makes his way through the smoke in the attempt to rescue her, he notices a million dollars in cash that she'd obviously been saving for the past 50 years. She'd collapsed while trying to retrieve it. The fire is approaching its zenith. He knows that he only has one chance to save either the money or the elderly woman who is apparently unconscious. He thinks "maybe she is already dead and this money is God's way of rewarding me for being a good person." Noble motives are like fresh milk. They "go bad" if not preserved properly and turn sour when placed in the midst of too much heat.

Before we can talk about solving the problems of Black and oppressed people, we must first discuss the critical importance of motive, intent and sincerity.

Sincerity is the key element if you wish to help the people of God. It is your motive that gives you your momentum. Just as toxins can enter into the pure bloodstream of a human being and make him or her sick, the pure motive of a good person can be toxified and cause the ultimate demise of a worthy endeavor. The problem with Black people is that we have too many ill-motivated leaders who "talk Black, live White and think Green." However , this chapter is not about them; it's about you and I.

Every child is born in a state of sincerity. Every time he or she cries, smiles or throws a tantrum; it is sincere. At some point in the child's development it learns how to utilize those smiles, tears and tantrums to manipulate situations and circumstances to achieve short-term goals. The hope is that we will outgrow those behaviors as adults and become spiritually mature. Unfortunately, it gets worse before it gets better; making it increasingly difficult to find sincere people in today's world.

Have you ever been inspired to join a church, mosque, organization, fraternity or sorority, but encountered some difficulty once you dedicated yourself to that cause or organization? Sometimes disunity, disorganization, fussing and fighting, mismanagement and an overall betrayal of the general objective of the organization can disappoint you to the point where you want to leave. It is at that moment that you must meditate and collect your thoughts about why you joined the organization in the first place.

I know people who went to law school with a sincere desire to make change. But once they graduated, passed the bar and began to practice law, they immediately run into a criminal justice system that vehemently resists change. In an effort to keep pace with the society, their desire to make change soon turns into a desire to make dollars. In the end, they may retain some moderate wealth, but usually at the price of being unfulfilled. How about the married couple that says "til death do us part" at the ceremony, but it does not last past the honeymoon. Too often we start off with a sincere and noble motive in our endeavors, but end up frustrated and abandon the goal. What happened? We've allowed negative forces and circumstances to tamper with our sincerity.

The Honorable Minister Louis Farrakhan teaches that "anything of value has a difficulty factor attached to it." How is this relevant to the subject of activism and the salvation of an oppressed people? If you wish to serve Black people you have to love them completely and believe in God's power to put them on top. The scripture says that "the last shall be first." However this will not take place without a fight. Let me be frank; you will run into difficulty in any attempt to help Black people. Never let the struggle poison the bloodstream of your motive.

Sincerity to the soul is much like the chin to a boxer. It must be protected at all costs if you are to finish the fight. My boxing trainer taught me that there are nerves found in the chin that are so sensitive that one blow can end a fight in a split second. The same goes for us all who strive for true success; especially those of us who seek to help in the cause of the resurrection of Black people and humanity in general. We must always be in the moment, remembering why we do what we do. We must never forget what brought tears to our eyes and made us want to help in this cause. We must do more than just look beyond our people's faults, we must see their needs and offer help with sincerity. We must, at all costs, protect the sincere motive that God gave us when we said that we wanted to be helpers in a cause that is bigger than us all.

Reflect on the best part of self; the self with no ulterior motive. We all have it within; it's just buried under our need for money, ego-edification, recognition, high position, sex and other forms of excess. Don't just go through the motions. Stay in the moment. Remain cognizant of why you do what you do no matter how insignificant the task. Sincerity allows us access to the power of God. Keep your hands up and your chin down. Pray for clarity and sincerity, work from your heart and watch God do extraordinary things through us Ordinary people.

Get involved in your community A.S.A.P. Do not get involved to be seen, do it so that the poor may be served. There is no amount of gold underneath the Earth that is more valuable than the heart of gold of a servant. As for the good Samaritan in the first paragraph; he concluded that saving the elder's life was the thing to do. Stealing her money was not. His reward was deposited into his soul; not his bank account. Always fight like hell to protect your sincerity.

CHAPTER 3

10 RESOLUTIONS FOR A

REVOLUTION

"He who refuses to discipline himself boycotts his own success." – @DericMuhammad

A wise mentor of mine used to tell me that there is no such thing as a "new" year if you do the same things you did the year before. It is just a continuation of the same agenda, schedule, way of life and way of thinking. In order to classify January 1st as the first day of the new year, you have to do something "new." If the only thing that changes in your life is the number on your calendar, we may as well wish you a happy "last year."

If we reflect on 2014 and realize that it was a near mirror of 2013, then it was not quite a new year. If we'll be honest, many of us have not had a new year in many years. The current social and economic challenges that we face in this country should force us to step outside of our comfort zone, challenge our fears and do something to better our condition.

We can all agree that the old way of doing things has failed us. The year 2013 was highlighted by something that was new to us all. Barack H. Obama became the first Black President of the United States of America to be reelected for a second term. If that cannot be classified as "new" then nothing else can.

Before the Black community can help anyone, we must first help ourselves. Here are 10 resolutions that I believe will help make the Black community a stronger community.

1. Stop Black-On-Black Violence and Murder.

2. Learn the difference between spirituality and religion. Strive to become a more spiritual community where neighbors pray together as much as they party together.

3. Eat to Live. Improper diet is generational and so are the illnesses that kill us as a result of our diet. Our forefathers ate certain foods on the plantation, because they had no choice. Why are we still eating the same foods 459 years later? Healthcare starts at home.

4. Each ONE Teach ONE (Mentor Neighborhood Youth). We have to mentor based on the talent and

interest of our young people. Link Black professionals with young brothers from the hood.

5. Natural Disaster Preparedness. Every year we are caught off guard during hurricane season. We seem to always be at the end of the line for government assistance after a natural disaster. This year we must put ourselves at the front of the line. The way to do that is to be better prepared.

6. Build and patriotically support Black-owned businesses that supply the needs of our community

7. Save your money. Stop spending money on unnecessary luxuries that you cannot afford. Mr. Gucci says you have to pay him hundreds of dollars in order to wear his name on your purse. He makes billions and sends his children to get the best education so that our children end up coming to them for a job.

8. Develop a political agenda. Support local, state and federal candidates that pledge allegiance to that agenda and politically punish them if they fail to keep their word.

9. Study Black history year-round. Make sure your

children know who they are and where they come from.

10. The Golden Rule: treat others the way you want to be treated.

These are just a few thoughts that, if executed, could equal a truly "new" year for the Black community.

CHAPTER 4

THE FIDDLER FACTOR

In Alex Haley's historic account of slavery in America "Roots," an unforgettable character named "Fiddler" plays an interesting role on the plantation. Fiddler was an entertainer, comedian, dealmaker, and peacemaker who, through the sheer force of his personality, kept the slaves calm and the slave master "grinning from ear to ear." Fiddler was the quintessential "plantation politician" who understood the art of saying all the right things in order to keep the peace and keep the crumbs falling from the slave master's table.

Just as every slave plantation had its own version of a "Fiddler," every Black community in modern-day America has a Black elected official who does the bidding of the rich and powerful while paying supreme lip service to his or her constituents. At no time have we had so many Black elected officials in office and at no time have they collectively been so powerless. Imagine squeezing a black berry only to find it filled with white juice. So it is with many Black elected officials. If you squeeze them hard enough you will find that they are filled with White ideas, White agendas and unparalleled fear.

The day after President Barack Obama secured the Democratic nomination for the presidency of the United States he did not go to Harlem, his hometown Chicago or any Black community for that matter. He didn't stop by his alma mater Harvard or any other place where his hard core supporters worked their tails off to get him nominated. Instead of busying himself thanking the majority, he paid a visit to a small minority. He went to Israel.

Why would the first Black man to be nominated for the American presidency make his first stop in the Jews' self-proclaimed homeland? It is likely because he felt that he could go no further without the proverbial "thumbs up" from the Jewish community. He had to pledge allegiance to Israel's flag before he could pledge allegiance to America's as her president. He was following the course of the vast majority of Black politicians who fear the Jewish lobby more than they fear the Black vote.

Earl Hilliard was a celebrated Congressman from the state of Alabama. A Morehouse graduate, he was elected to Congress in 1992, the first Black man to represent Alabama in the U.S. Congress. In 2001 he dared to vote against a bill funding increases in military support to Israel. This angered the Jewish lobby who then demonized him in the media and used its economic prowess to fund his opponent in the next election. Hilliard lost his seat.

Because he refused to sign off on a "pledge of allegiance" to Israel during a time when Israel was committing war crimes against the Palestinians, he was strategically unseated.

What about Congresswoman Cynthia McKinney of Atlanta, Georgia? She was labeled an anti-Semite for merely speaking her mind. A candidate was recruited to run against her and was well-financed by the Jewish community. Many Jews switched political parties just so they could vote against her and they succeeded in forcing her out of office. It is situations like Hilliard's and McKinney's that instill absolute fear in Black politicians. And wherever there is fear, control is not far behind.

If I've heard it once I've heard it a billion times. "Black people fought, bled and died for the right to vote", is what we say. But how effective is our vote if the people we elect are controlled by an element that had a historical hand in our oppression? As stated in the Nation of Islam Historical Research Department's book titled: "The Secret Relationship between Blacks and Jews" Vol. 2. "Jews were about twice as likely to be slave owners as the average White southerner." This same powerful book makes the case that the very Jim Crow laws that Dr. King and others marched to change were actually put in place by Jews in the south.

So let me get this straight. Jewish people bankrolled the Civil Rights Organizations that marched to uproot the Jim Crow laws that Jews put in place so that we could secure the right to vote for Black politicians that would eventually end up under Jewish control. You have got to be kidding me.

It is sickening to me the way Black elected officials genuflect and kowtow at the mere mention of AIPAC and the Jewish lobby. It's unconscionable to see our elected officials pledging allegiance to Israel, yet turning their noses up at Africa. Black congressmen are lauded for their support of Israel, yet have to go jail for protesting a humanitarian crisis in the Sudan. Jewish forces should not have more control over Black politicians than the Black community and if this is the case we need to face the music and change the tune.

The other side to this dynamic serves as an indictment on us as a people. We don't pool our resources as we should and financially back good candidates. The Jewish community can always use the might of their unified dollars to bully our elected officials into becoming cheerleaders for "all things Jewish." The same is true for corporate America. If we are going to participate in the political process as a people we must do so from a position of great strength.

Brothers like Hilliard should be free to be men and vote the conscious of the community without having to suffer a targeted attack like the one that removed him from his seat.

We must give supreme political protection to strong politicians who are unafraid to represent our legitimate interests and issue pink slips to those who compromise our aims and aspirations in order to please our former slave masters. Politics is war. And we ought to be sick and tired of sending soldiers to the battlefield who fight for everyone else's interest, except for their senders'.

CHAPTER 5

Black Power...White Dollars

Does Corporate Sponsorship Weaken the Voice of Black Leadership?

A wise man once said, "whoever controls your food can control your revolution". There was a time when the enemies of justice saw a movement that represented a potential threat to their power they would do their best to stop it. Nowadays they don't try and stop it. **THEY JUST FINANCE IT.**

One of the formulas for maintaining White supremacy has always been to keep the wise and fearless revolutionaries from the necessary resources to support a revolution. Nobody understands this better than the American government whose war chest is the biggest chest on the government body. If you keep the wise man poor he has very few outlets to manifest his wisdom and make it into a reality. If you keep the rich man ignorant then he is no threat to the powers that be. This is especially true with Black athletes and entertainers. The day that strong, sincere Black leaders and organizations are blessed with the collective support of Black wealth it will be a marriage that divorces us from our dependency on the White dollar.

For example, in June of 2008, one of our great civil rights stalwarts, Reverend Al Sharpton, made a deal with the federal government that cooled the flames of an ongoing criminal investigation into his personal financial affairs and that of The National Action Network (NAN) that he commandeers out of New York City. He and the NAN were a couple of million behind in taxes, but were also accused of everything from destroying financial records to exchanging big dollars for civil rights "ghetto passes".

The investigation disclosed some of Sharpton's corporate sponsors who contribute hundreds of thousands to NAN's coffers annually. Some included Anheuser-Busch, Walmart, Continental Airlines and a host of others. As a matter of fact, according to the New York Post nearly 50 companies and labor unions sponsored the NAN's annual conference in April. The feds described Al as a paid consultant who assists some of these companies in settling race-related legal disputes with Black employees and customers. Rev. Al called it a retaliatory witch hunt. This is probably true. The FBI has a well-recorded history of infiltrating Black organizations seeking to destabilize them.

Also in June of 2008, the NAACP, the oldest civil rights organization in America, reportedly had to dip into millions of its financial reserves and close all of its regional offices due to budgetary shortfalls. Many do not know that the NAACP was co-founded by Whites in 1909. As such, it is not surprising that they receive monies from corporate entities and huge donations from White people who support the cause.

Question: Does White corporate sponsorship weaken the strength of the voice of those who claim to lead us? Can you believe in "Black Power" when it's brought to you by Chrysler Corporation"? Does corporate sponsorship represent a payoff and a promise that the company never has to worry about a picket line or protest outside its headquarters? Is the civil rights movement buried in the budget of some of these Fortune 500 Companies?

As a community activist I am always asked the question; "how do you make your money?" Once you reach a certain level of activism it becomes pretty clear that the bank may not hire you. But, revolutionaries and civil rights warriors are not excused from feeding their families. Our bills come with the same regularity as the people that we represent.

Both Dr. Martin Luther King Jr. and Malcolm X were killed in the line of duty and both died virtually poor. Marcus Garvey also died poor. I sometimes wonder if the expectation of Black people dictate that their leaders be penniless in order to prove their nobility. If that is the case, we have not evolved far enough as a people to understand what it takes to make real revolutionary progress.

I am not knocking corporate sponsorship of Black organizations. As a matter of fact I encourage it. Black people are collectively spending billions of dollars annually with Nike, Mercedes-Benz, Target, Ralph Lauren, etc. We, as consumers, make them wealthy and powerful with dollars that we don't have. They should all be made to give back to the Black community just as they give back to other communities that make them strong and viable. So you have corporate sponsors competing for the Black dollar and Black organizations competing for corporate sponsorship. The problem comes in when we bend over backwards to be accepted by them and compromise the principles of freedom, justice and equality in the process.

If we accept corporate America's dollars on corporate America's terms then we have become hirelings who are not worthy to lead our people. If we disassociate ourselves from other organizations in our community for fear of what "Mr. Kentucky Fried Chicken" will say then we have lost the testicular fortitude necessary to forge the way to freedom.

The best approach would be for Black people to spend less money with these companies and use it to support our own Black organizations. We must have the collective intelligence to realize that every time we spend outside of our community our dollars are used to support the agenda of another people. Every person within eye and earshot of this article should make a pledge to donate to a worthy Black organization or cause within the next 12 months. If we support our own then there is a better chance that they will maintain the "bass in their voices" while representing our best interests. This is also true for good Black politicians, but we will deal with that in a future article.

Remember, " freedom is not free". We cannot expect to get to the promise land on Pharaoh's chariot. Support your own and hold them accountable. If we don't then corporate America will.

CHAPTER 6

The Difference between a Black business and a "Negro" business

" Do not criticize what you do not patronize"
@DericMuhammad

Over 300 years of chattel slavery in America totally destroyed Black people's natural desire to do-for-self. After Abraham Lincoln issued the executive order known as the Emancipation Proclamation, Black slaves were declared free, yet were given few opportunities to make a living to feed their families. Many slaves immediately returned to the plantations of their slave masters because they did not know what else to do.

For a long time, slaves were forbidden to read or write. But the slave master made certain they knew how to count. How else were they to keep up with their daily cotton quotas on the plantation? Many slaves utilized the skills they mastered as plantation workers and began doing business for themselves. As a matter of fact, many slaves had already started businesses and became strong enough economically to purchase the freedom for some of their family members. A price was paid before Black people were able to do business in the United States of America.

Our businesses thrived in this country when we understood the urgency of moments in time like "Reconstruction," the Great Depression and Jim Crow. We knew that if we did not support one another we could not survive. Prior to integration, Whites refused to do business with us.

These days it is difficult to keep a Black business open. According to statistics, Black-owned businesses open and close faster than businesses owned by any other ethnic group in America.

I remember attending a community event with a Houston U.S. Congressman. I excused myself to a nearby Black-owned restaurant to use its restroom. As I attempted to exit the restroom, I was hit with a painful reality. I was locked inside. After about fifteen minutes of trying to "break free" I, embarrassingly, called someone from our entourage who sent an employee from the restaurant to come and rescue me.

I heard the footsteps coming down the corridor and I was relieved until I saw a silver butter knife slid underneath the door. "Jimmy it with the knife", he said. No, no, no... right there in the center. You almost got it." There was nothing else for me to do but accept his coaching in order to free myself from the restroom.

While I will not divulge the name of this establishment, I shared this experience to expose how many Black establishments fail miserably to provide goods, services and amenities in a way that keeps customers coming back. These same businesses complain that we somehow believe the White man's ice is colder.

I often hear horror stories about how hard-working people pay Black contractors to do a job that never gets finished. You sometimes show up at a coffee shop or restaurant and they are closed when they are supposed to be open. Too often, we say that we will have a service completed by a certain date and fail to deliver. Many Black businesses close themselves down.

Now let's take a closer look at the Black business patron. Too often good Black businesses cringe at doing business with our own people, because we are always looking for "the hook-up." There are good Black contractors who finish jobs and then are paid with a rubber check! We show up at the Black coffee shop just to use the internet and then go buy a latte from Starbucks. Sometimes Black business owners just give up or move to the suburbs because doing business in the 'hood, proves to be too challenging.

In all fairness, these business snafus are not limited to Black businesses. You can go anywhere in town and find poor customer service. However, if we are to survive during these economically challenging times, we must get back to the basics of nation building and self-development. We must support Black businesses that are serious about doing business and eliminate businesses that poison the water that we all must drink from.

In order to do business, we must show character. We must open and close when we say we will open and close.

We must treat the Black customer with the same regard that we would treat a dignitary. It does not matter whether the brother or sister is spending $5 or $5,000. If you treat us like kings and queens, we will return to do business with you once again. We need Black business bureaus and Black chambers of commerce in every one of our communities. We must be honest and trustworthy in our dealings with one another. Even when we make errors, we must quickly correct ourselves and move on. These are a few keys to the survival of Black business in America.

CHAPTER 7

The Culture of Silence: The Molestation of Black Boys

"They say I'm wasting my time ministering to young Black males. I say they're wasting their time talking to me." - @DericMuhammad

They play tough positions on professional football teams, hold high political offices, supervise construction shifts and preach from the pulpits of spiritual places of worship. They are leaders of street organizations, captains of corporate industry, hard-core rap stars and short-order cooks. Who are they? They are Black males who were molested as boys.

While the rape and molestation of females has spawned a plethora of preventive programs and inspired international dialogue, the ever increasing rape of young boys is still a taboo subject. Statistics say that the abuse of young boys is on the rise, but I wonder how accurate those stats could be given the fact that most men who have been abused would never discuss or admit it.

As a Black male in America I have never had a friend, associate or family member confess that they were sexually abused. As an activist, I have assisted many with different types of criminal cases, social issues and problems. However, I have never received a phone call from a male stating that he had been sexually violated. It can be likened to the proverbial bowling ball underneath the living room rug; you can't see it, but you can't stop tripping over it.

How many Black men walk the streets of America suffering from such an unfortunate past? How many of them fear society's ridicule if they should choose to talk about it? How many sick molesters of boys depend on this very fear to remain unpunished and continue their victimization of the innocent? And how much of financial resources, time, energy and organization is being invested in programs that identify, support and promote the healing of men who were molested as children?

Movie director/actor/entrepreneur Tyler Perry personally went on record about being abused as a young boy. Hundreds of news reports quoted Perry's sentiments about a deceased man whose family asked that Perry pay for his funeral. Perry reportedly refused, but later regretted it. He said that there would have been something powerful about burying the man that molested him.

Whether people agreed with Perry's sentiments or not, you have to respect his courageous address of his past in hopes of inspiring someone else's future. Years ago Oprah Winfrey went public about details of her experience being molested as a young girl. The world showered her with sympathy and rallied around her in support. I wonder if Mr. Perry has received the same outpour considering he is a man. God forbid the same world that rallied around Oprah secretly sees Mr. Perry as a weak human being because of his reported past.

While the Catholic Church has for years been marred by scandal on top of scandal surrounding this issue, I contend that child molestation has no religion. While it happens every day in the Black community, it is very seldom discussed. Too often the pain and embarrassment of the community is made to be more important than the pain of the victim. While we are able to put on a good face for the community in the end it comes back to haunt us.

Psychologists say that boys who have been molested tend to suffer from depression, repressed anger, emotional confusion and fear. Many suffer from identity crises, drug addiction, alcoholism and the inability to maintain good relationships. Many go on to become molesters themselves repeating the very horrific acts that inflicted such great pain in their lives. Some end up committing suicide leaving their families with unanswered questions and visible teardrops.

While it should be clear that we as a community must do more to protect our young girls from rape and molestation, we must not forget to sharpen our collective eye to protect our boys. We must be mindful of their surroundings at all times and be careful whose hands we leave them in.

Parents must teach little boys regarding appropriate contact versus inappropriate contact with others. This conversation is no longer just reserved for young girls.

If you are a man who has suffered this kind of abuse, seek refuge in God for He is the master healer of all wounds. Be encouraged and know that the abuse from your past makes you no less of a man. As a matter of fact, your strength to persevere in the name of God makes you greater than most men. Much respect to Tyler Perry.

CHAPTER 8

Message to Teen-Aged Mothers

"How you grew up does not have to dictate how you end up." -@ DericMuhammad

Mavis Jackson was 19 years old and pregnant again. Since she already had two children, abortion seemed like a plausible option. But despite the fact that society looked down on teen-aged mothers back then, she decided to have that child anyway. Truth is… you are reading these words because my mother, Mavis Jackson, made a critical decision to birth me. I am proud to say that I was that third child.

Now do not get me wrong. As the father of two daughters, ages 9 and 13, I am NOT advocating teen-aged pregnancy. Nor am I glorifying it. I believe that every young female should be taught her intrinsic value as well as how to maintain her virtue. We are literally "watch-men" over the minds and bodies of the girls in our families. We must ensure that they mature into young ladies who are well respected, completely protected and thoroughly educated. They must know beyond a shadow of any doubt that it is crucial for them to keep their knees closed and hearts open until a worthy man comes along who will accept full responsibility for their continued care and development. Remember, a man who truly loves you is less concerned with the shape of your body and more concerned with the shape of your mind.

Our chief desire is that all of our young girls remain virgins until they have grown up and have married. Unfortunately, most of them don't make it. Because our children are over exposed to sexual innuendos, information and imagery, it is very difficult to keep them focused. I am not saying that it is impossible, but it certainly is no easy task. Many of our young girls start having sexual intercourse before time, because their bodies develop faster than their minds. Subsequently, some end up pregnant and have babies. The million dollar question then becomes, **"How are we going to treat them?"**

I stand resolute in the fact that we should discourage "babies from having babies. However, once a teen gives birth to a child, that child, in turn, becomes a member of our community. And every child should be treated with as much love, care and compassion as possible. It is foolish to discriminate against a child because of the circumstances of his or her birth. It is equally irrational to stand in judgment of a teen-aged girl who decides to preserve rather than end the life of a child. Like it or not, both the baby and the mother still belong to us as a community. We must not sentence them to hell through insensitive and tactless behavior.

This editorial was inspired by a counseling session I had today with a 17 year-old mother who had been vilified by her teacher. When she told him that she did not understand her geometry work, he replied loud enough for everyone to hear, "evidently you don't understand nothing but a penis" (only he did not use the word penis). Needless to say, the entire class thought it was funny. How could a man charged with the education of students be so careless with the mother of a one-year-old child? I literally wanted to choke the hell out of this man! Listen to me loud and clear, the minds of young girls are shaped by the things that men say to them. And if we in the Ministry of Justice have anything to do with it, that man will not be teaching geometry much longer. (I'm still livid!)

We must do our best to prevent teen-aged pregnancy in our community. However, once the baby arrives, we must embrace that baby as a gift from God. Since all life comes from Him, all children are legitimate. No young girl winds up pregnant by herself. As such, we must make sure both the young mother and father learn to be good parents; and encourage them to be better and do better. Anything else is hypocritical and non-productive.

I don't know about you, but I love all Black babies. I don't care what circumstances they were born under.

I am grateful that I was in a position to tell that young girl that she should never hold her head in shame. We would have preferred that she waited, but since she did not, we accept her baby as a blessing. I shared the circumstances surrounding my birth, and how, by God's grace, things turned out fine. Some of the greatest human beings in the world were products of teen pregnancies; and her baby was no different. I told her that the Jews of the Bible questioned the "legitimacy" of the birth of Jesus, but that did not stop Him from becoming the Christ.

I wonder what my mother had to endure as a 19 year old with three children in the seventies. I appreciate her for the price she paid to ensure our success. Our struggle made me compassionate toward young mothers like the one I ministered to today. Although people may have looked down on my mother because of me, I assure you before it's over, they will look up to her because of me.

CHAPTER 9

A Letter to the "Half-Dressed Queen"

"Teach the children WORK ethic...not TWERK ethic". — @Deric Muhammad

During the spring and summer months, women wear less clothing. While some men may consider this a summer perk, they feel vastly different when their own daughters emulate the same. You can predictably watch his *kool-aid* smile turn into a wrinkled-faced frown. It is because they realize that men just like themselves are entertained by the revealing clothing of an attractive woman. And they do not want their daughters viewed in that manner. I'm only keeping it real.

The way you dress says a lot about the way you think. I am not advocating we judge individuals by material things, but it is true that we communicate ideas through styles.

I remember a close friend telling me the true story of how he picked his uncle up from the bus station after he was released from prison.

The year was 1994 and he'd been in prison for 12 years.

As he rode through the downtown streets of Houston, he kept saying that he couldn't believe how many prostitutes there were walking the streets during daylight hours.

My friend had to tell him that those were normal women; not prostitutes. The styles had changed so drastically while he was imprisoned that he mistook a regular sister on her way to work for a "working girl."

I am as natural as a natural man can get. I love the sight of a beautiful woman just like the next man. But where do we draw the line, when 12-year-old girls who have the shapely bodies of grown women are walking around in skirts so short you can see their undergarments?

If a man sees that little girl from a distance he cannot delineate whether she is 12 or 25. And that grown man will make a u-turn right in the middle of the street to get a closer look at a 12-year-old baby. But once the man sees the middle-school uniform the girl is wearing, he will turn yet again and ask the Lord for forgiveness. Other times, we are not so lucky.

This letter is an appeal to teen-aged girls to make sure that you are communicating the right message when you leave out of the house. The absence of the father in the home sometimes leaves a young daughter craving the attention of the male gender. When her female body parts begin to develop, and she notices that boys are taking interest, it is not unusual to like the attention. If not taught properly, she will desire to wear clothing that accentuate the body parts she is most proud of, such as her breasts or her backside. While this may warrant her some "very temporary" attention, in the long run it will only hurt her.

Young ladies, I must be honest. As a man, I know how men and boys think about the women who dress to attract men with their bodies. Males LIKE women who dress provocatively, but males RESPECT females who dress respectfully. If you think I'm lying go to a job interview in a mini-dress and platform heels. You will not get that job. That is unless it is in a strip club.

When a business seeks to attract the attention of potential customers, they develop advertisements. They promote products that generate the interests of certain kinds of customers. As a young lady, every time you get dressed, you are a walking billboard. What kind of customers are you attracting?

Any boy or young man who is only drawn to your body and physical beauty is a person who is not worthy of you. You must be taught how to display your intelligence, talent and personality in a way that will appeal to a respectable young man.

Any young lady can get a male to stop and pay attention to her body. It takes a special young lady who is secure enough in herself to cause a man to respect her mind. Parents should responsibly mentor and teach young girls how to present themselves like young ladies.

When appropriately dressed, girls become a magnet for rapists and child molesters. A study showed that most repeat-offender rapists look for female victims wearing clothing that can be easily removed. So when you are walking the streets in your mini-dresses, there are sick men watching.

I want you to know that you are too beautiful and intelligent to walk around dressed this way. Do not allow the shape of your behind to speak louder than your mind. We must respect and protect the Black female, but she must first be taught how to respect herself. While self-respect starts with the way you think, it is reflected in the way you dress. Put some clothes on young lady!

The Black man has got your back, but I'm going to have to ask you cover it up first.

CHAPTER 10

Teen Lesbianism

There is a day that every father dreads. It is, perhaps, his worst nightmare. The day when his daughter comes home and says, "Daddy I have a boyfriend". His heart skips three beats, his throat gets dry and he immediately goes to the garage and starts cleaning that 'ole rusty 38' pistol.

Nowadays, little girls' parents are more relieved than rattled by the traditional boyfriend announcement. It sure beats the new nightmare that too many are having to endure when their daughters come home and boldly declare, "Daddy I have a girlfriend".

Teen lesbianism in the Black community has become rampant. It is becoming the "elephant in the room" that nobody wants to acknowledge. Ignored or not, that elephant is getting bigger with each passing day. It is not uncommon to see school-aged girls sporting sagging jeans, wave caps, fade haircuts and mean-mugged facial expressions. While the uniform does not necessitate lesbianism, the girl wearing the short skirt whose hand she is holding usually does.

I remember seeing a couple with their young child at Houston's Hermann Park having what appeared to be a family outing. The child called out "daddy look at me". But when daddy turned around, it was all too obvious that *daddy* was a not a male, but rather a female. In my estimation, that little baby girl was on her way to sure confusion.

Now let me preface further commentary by officially stating that I am not a homophobic. I am aware that this is a sensitive subject for many and I do not wish to be mislabeled. This kind of issue is also often considered a political editorial "no-no". But if we, as a community, do not face our problems squarely we can never create solutions wisely.

I believe, we as Black men have failed our women miserably. Our mental, spiritual, psychological and emotional condition has deteriorated the hopes of some Black women so badly that being with a woman as opposed to a man is appealing. Much to my dismay, there is an unprecedented number of women exercising that option. The mistreatment of the Black female has so disgusted some of our sisters that they are turning to one another for comfort, consolation and companionship.

This has been a fact for years in the hood, but never have we seen so many engage in this lifestyle at such an early age.

It is a scientific, biological and social fact that "opposites attract". You don't have to teach a female to be attracted to the male species; her God-given nature dictates that attraction. However, when that natural inclination is reversed, we must discover the reason why. Often when a young girl is sexually molested, (sometimes by her own father), she develops general and innate hatred for men. If she is negatively impacted when she witnesses her mother suffer extreme abuse from a husband or boyfriend, she will make a conscious decision to never allow a man to violate her that way. Young women who have taken the course of lesbianism are often victims of rape, molestation or extreme abuse. But you cannot pre-judge, misjudge or improperly assess her situation if you would like to help her.

In order to solve a problem you must get to the root cause of the problem. Teen Lesbianism is not necessarily the problem. There is a general deterioration of the social fabric in our society and this is the by-product of a sex-crazed world that uses sex to sell everything from grits to garbage cans. It is the direct result of the conspiracy to destroy the Black male; and our willingness to be co-conspirators in our own demise. Also it is the direct result of the culture that degrades women as tools of pleasure, and influences our young boys to treat our young girls like things; not like queens.

My impetus for this short message is to create a dialogue about the hurt our young girls are enduring. Many mothers and grandmothers are heartbroken by this epidemic and don't know what to do. The first thing that we must do is to come out of denial.

We have to pay closer attention to our daughters. There is no point in acting as if it could never happen to you, because it just might. Do not allow your young daughters to keep company with strange men. In fact, they should never be alone with men. We have to guard our daughters and protect them from the abuse of men, even if it costs us our lives. This will lessen the chances of teen lesbianism infiltrating our families.

If indeed you see some of the tell-tale signs, do not ignore them. Sit down and talk with your daughter. Try and find out the root cause of her decision. Do not overreact by becoming physically or verbally abusive. You may discover that she was raped or molested, and hidden it from you for years. If you are blessed to find the cause then you should seek professional or spiritual help for her. Let the healing process begin!

I even encourage our clergy – those who preach the Gospel, to address this subject on Sunday morning. Not one of us can afford to miss this opportunity for fear of an economic backlash. Rather, we must fear the heaviness of God's wrath if we do not speak the truth that can save our people. We must use the healing power of the Word of God to touch the hearts and minds of these young girls. Instead of condemning them, we must minister with love to their confusion. **Remember, let he who is without sin cast the first stone.**

We must also develop stronger laws that punish those who violate little girls. We must teach the value of the female to every young boy so that young girls will see hope in them; not despair. The bottom line is men must be men. We will see a difference when we, as Black men, take our rightful place in our communities.

CHAPTER 11

DOUBLE DUTY

The Black Woman's Struggle Raising Boys Alone

"The more people depend on you, the more you have to depend on God." – *@DericMuhammad*

It is only a matter of time before Hallmark designs and manufactures a Father's Day Card for Black women. They would fly off of the shelves in the Black community. It would be difficult for us as a community to protest given the fact that we have helped create the market for it.

God, in His infinite wisdom, has set up a system for the family structure. He gives every child, male and female, a mother and a father. Both parents are by nature made to fulfill their roles so that the child receives what he or she needs to grow into their full potential according to the plan of a wise God. So the presence of a father in the life of a child is not only a human need; it is a human right.

The Black nation is hemorrhaging from within, because so many Black boys have been denied this human right. There is a deep, scathing, internally scarring pain on the inside of us as Black men, because we have felt the sting of rejection from our fathers. Every young Black male who feels "dissed" by his biological father sees himself as a victim of injustice. He is hurt. He is bitter.

This injustice could very well create a mental imbalance that careens out of control into savage behavior. The young Black male is "Fatherless and Furious." If we intend to stop the violence in our communities, we must be ready to address the pathology of the problem and how it turns into the disease of self-hatred.

While it takes two to make a baby boy, it seems like the Black woman has been left with the burden of being the king maker. Black men are showing up in the bedroom, but not showing up in the delivery room. Too often, this drama is played out in some court room. It is because the lessons about life that fathers are supposed to teach their sons are being taught and misinterpreted by the streets, television, rap stars, etc.

The woman is endowed by God to be a loving

nurturer. She has been given a feminine quality that serves as a source of support for her son who will one day be a young man. Too often mother has to step outside of herself (her nature) to play the role of father. It is a role for which she is not designed, but has no other choice than to fulfill. This is mentally, spiritually, physically, financially and even clinically an unfair burden to her. Men, we must do a better job of helping her. The stress of being both mother and father to the Black male has probably taken an incalculable toll on the health of Black women in this nation.

Raising Black boys in a world like this is difficult enough for two parents. But when a woman has to do it alone, it's like playing a doubles match of tennis against Venus and Serena Williams alone and without a partner. Impossible, you say?

If you are a single female who is shouldering the responsibility of raising a son alone, take courage. There are a large number of great men who were raised by mothers. We would gain certain advantages by studying the mothers of great men like Minister Farrakhan who grew up without a father in the home. What did Mother Farrakhan do to ensure her son became the man that God intended?

Many other brilliant and successful Black men, such as Barack Obama, Rev. Jesse Jackson and others grew up void of a father and became great helpers in the cause of our people.

They are witnesses to the fact that great sons can be produced through great mothers.

If you will, allow me to draw your attention to Mary, the mother of Jesus who was a single Black woman who raised a son. Some will argue that Mary was NOT a single mother, because God was the father of Jesus. Just as God was with Mary, he is also with you. And if God is with you, even Venus and Serena couldn't beat you in a doubles match (smile).

Although it looked as if Mary was by herself; she wasn't. Every single mother must adopt a similar attitude. It may look like she is by herself, but she is not. We can steer our young boys in a better direction, stop the bleeding in our community and start the building of our community with God's help. But the Black woman should not have to do it alone. Black men must take some responsibility for the misdirected anger that kills our young brothers. We must accept our God-given duty to raise our young Black boys.

CHAPTER 12

Black on Black Killing:
A Modern tool of White Supremacy

Imagine approaching a man in a Ku Klux Klan uniform from behind. You can clearly see the white sheeted uniform, but you can't quite make out his face. The very sight of such a symbol of White supremacy is enough to anger any Black man. But what happens when he turns around and you realize that the Klan member is a Black man?

The very thought of seeing a Black man in a KKK uniform sends a sane mind into a state of confusion. What self-respecting human being would subscribe to an ideology that seeks his very extermination? Wouldn't the law of self-preservation prevent a Black man from wearing such an outfit? Think about it. What worm joins a bird gang?

No sane Black man would voluntarily join the KKK, Skinheads or any neo-Nazi movement. I am sure the Grand Wizard wouldn't allow it. However, with Black on Black murder hitting record numbers in inner-cities across the country, I wonder how many of us already joined up without realizing it.

White supremacy is rooted in the belief that Whites are superior to non-Whites. Black people historically have suffered more than any other people under this philosophy. The Honorable Elijah Muhammad, in his illuminating book "Message to the Blackman" taught that the White race came to be through a systematic, scientific formula called grafting. The rule was to kill the darker people and save the lighter people. To this day, that formula is the means by which the preservation of the White race is attempted.

Since the elimination of Black people is a key component of the maintenance of the ideology of White Supremacy, have we become secret agents of the Ku Klux Klan and other White Supremacists groups? *Could a Black man who kills another Black man be considered one of Hitler's children?* In the past, these groups have predicted a "race war" in which they would kill Blacks wholesale. But it seems that is no longer necessary today, because we are already killing one another wholesale.

There has been a reported rise in the number of those joining White Supremacist groups operating in the United States. The meteoric rise to power of President Barack Obama has been cited as the probable cause and number one catalyst for recruitment. While this uprising of racial hate could be considered a threat to Black people, the biggest threat to our survival is self-annihilation and self-genocide via Black on Black murder.

The great comedian Dave Chapelle once performed a hilarious parody where he portrayed a blind Black man named Clayton Bigsby who was a leader in the Ku Klux Klan. This fictitious brother, who was born blind, taught White supremacy and sought the annihilation of his own people. It was not until he was coerced into taking off his head covering at a Klan rally that he found out who he was. It was a very funny show, but it was filled with symbolism.

Any man who seeks the annihilation of his own people is as blind as Clayton Bigsby. He does not know who he is and must be coerced into taking off the head covering of self-hatred and falsehood. Most of us who saw Dave Chapelle's parody laughed until our stomach muscles contracted, because the mere thought of a brother in a KKK uniform was ludicrous! But I ask the sobering question, what's worse; wearing a white sheet or killing a Black man?

I think that the sociopolitical ideology of White supremacy is dying a natural death. However, every time a Black man or woman commits fratricide, we give it mouth-to-mouth resuscitation. The Honorable Minister Louis Farrakhan has taught us that our unity and the display of Black excellence is the death knell of White supremacy. We can only be unified when we are able to resolve conflict among ourselves in a civilized and productive fashion without resulting to this nonproductive shedding of blood.

I would say that perpetrators of Black on Black violence and murder may not have joined the KKK, but they have certainly unwittingly joined their cause. We must work tirelessly to stop the violence in our communities. We must protest the brutality that we inflict on each other just as strongly as we protest racial injustice committed against us by law enforcement and others.

We can no longer afford to act as co-conspirators with White supremacy. Every funeral of ours is cause for celebration for our oppressors. Every time we teach a Black brother or sister the knowledge of self and others we facilitate the funeral for White world supremacy. We must make a conscious decision to never join the cause of those who lynched and burned our ancestors. "Use your mind instead of your nine". Stop the killing, now!!!"

CHAPTER 13

The Attracting Power of 'Gangs'
Why Churches and Community Organizations Should Study Them

This subject title has been very heavy on my heart for some time. So when I decided to write about it, I reached out to a very close friend of mine who lives in Chicago. He is a businessman who was a gang leader that turned his life around. Since I've never been in an organized gang, I decided that I should get some intimate perspectives about what attracted him and others to street organizations; a.k.a. 'gangs.'

After several unsuccessful attempts to reach him, I began to wonder what was wrong. "That's not like him…he usually return my calls right away", I thought. A few days later I received an email from his wife. My dear friend had just been murdered in his old neighborhood on the Westside. That Friday I was on a plane to Chicago to his memorial service. I've prefaced this subject with this vignette, because I believe that it speaks to the urgency concerning this particular discussion.

The National Gang Intelligence Center for the U.S. Justice Department reports that gang membership in the U.S. has swelled to nearly one million members. The report indicates that membership is up 200,000 since 2005 with some 900,000 gang members in local communities while 147,000 languish in prison. Depending on one's definition of a so-called gang member, I would have to assume the actual numbers may very well surpass their findings.

As a community we should be found studying the attracting power of these street organizations. There is an ever-increasing rise in the number of Black men gravitating towards so-called gangs. It would most certainly benefit the community at large to take another look at the methodology we are employing to capture the attention of our boys versus what actually seizes their interest?

The Honorable Elijah Muhammad taught his followers about the Law of Attraction. The formula he gave was very clear; opposites attract and likes repel. He taught us the history of a scientist born 20 miles from the holy city of Mecca. Apparently, while playing with two pieces of steel at the age of six, he discovered that one piece of steel had magnetic attraction and the other did not. He ultimately used this powerful law of attraction to draw thousands to himself and his teaching to complete an assignment that was written of him 8,400 years before his birth.

The law of attraction is not national, it is universal. It is at work even when we are asleep. The combination of poor socio-economic conditions and the break-up of families have created the perfect storm for so-called gang recruitment. Gang-mania in the U.S.A. is a direct by-product of deprived and disenfranchised communities. After coupling my conversations with many so-called gang-affiliated individuals with my own personal experience, I realized there are so many things that attract youth to so-called gangs that I can't fit it all into one editorial. However, here are some of our findings.

Communication—First of all, the leader of a street organization is not afraid to show up in the worst parts of the city. In many cases, they already live there. No church or street organization can ever expect to reach our youth if they are too afraid to go and minister to them "where they are."

It's not necessarily about whose words are more effective, it usually comes down to who is not afraid to step to them face to face.

Security—Statistics show that 70 percent of households in the Black community are headed by females. The absence of a father in the home creates an innate sense of natural insecurity in the Black male. When a recruit joins the gang he is happy to bond with other males who understand his plight. This ultimately translates into security from physical harm but it actually starts emotionally. Every church and/or organization must offer this to be successful in winning over our youth. We must offer emotional security that somehow also translates into physical security.

Transparency—Most young people see so-called gangs as organizations that "keep it real." They believe that even if the gang is involved in illicit activity at least they are not "faking it." Clearly, the best way to attract young people to churches and similar organizations is to sincerely practice what you preach. Hypocrisy is unattractive to young people.

Patriotism—The Black male is a soldier by nature. Our experience as a people in America has left such a sour taste in the mouths of our youth that many reject the government of America. So-called gangs give youth something to believe in and identify with, coupled with its very own unique culture. It is no coincidence that their bandanas are called "flags."

Financial Opportunity— Financial opportunities are scarce for young people growing up in urban America. When there is no food in the home and it is up to the youngster to fend for himself, so-called gang life is enticing. It doesn't matter that many of the activities for financial gain are not legal; the opportunity to feed and clothe himself and his younger siblings is appreciated. Every church, mosque and community organization must develop programs that create financial opportunities for youth.

I have been called crazy and out of touch for suggesting that we should study gangs. While everyone else is campaigning to wipe them out; this message and methodology proves not to be the solution. However, if we can humble ourselves and alter our approach, surely we can find the Answer to our Problem. When we change the way we look at a thing/situation, oftentimes the thing/situation changes.

CHAPTER 14

"Conflict Resolution: Reducing Black Male Violence"

"Everything you want out of life can be obtained through the cultivation of what you already have."
— *@DericMuhammad*

We live in a world full of conflict. The reason wars exist throughout the earth is because human beings refuse to sit down and resolve disagreements. Conflict is natural. You cannot live in this world without having a disagreement with your fellow man. However, conflict does not have to lead to violence or murder.

According to Webster's dictionary, a conflict is defined as a clash of ideas and/or interests. The human being is born into conflict. When a baby is born, the very lighting in the delivery room conflicts with the darkness of the womb where it lived for nine months. Sooner or later the newborn's eyes adjust to the power of light. This is termed "resolution" in the optical profession. Resolution is relative to one's ability to see clearly.

There are many forms of conflict within the Black community. There are conflicts in politics, religion, grass-roots organizations, fraternities, sororities, civic clubs, etc. The failure to successfully resolve conflicts that arise in marriage is what has contributed to the high rate of divorce. If we sincerely desire to see our youth iron out their differences, we as adults must lead the way

There are family conflicts that last for generations. We all have family members who don't "fool with" other family members. Some have literally refused to speak to blood relatives because of some trivial disagreement that took place more than ten years ago. Sometimes, they cannot even remember what the initial dispute was about.

Conflict among Young Black Males Most of the time, conflict among young Black males comes when someone feels they have been threatened, disrespected or violated. I have seen arguments over $10.00 turn into murder cases.

When two young males seem to be about to get at one another's throat, do your best to maneuver them into separate rooms. If a crowd forms, try to disperse it. Sometimes a big crowd can be like gas on the fire of an emerging fight. And if there are females in the crowd, males tend to feel they have even more to prove.

In most cases, you have to wait until both parties calm down before trying to talk about what happened. You can almost never resolve conflict while people are angry. Anger causes a loss of reasoning. Once things calm down, you should find a mediator that both parties RESPECT. It may be a teacher, coach or a well-respected parent. It may even be a highly intelligent classmate. Make sure the person is not going to take sides. Make sure the person is only interested in peace. This person can be called a "peacemaker."

Once you have found a respected mediator, the key is to get to the very root cause of the dispute. Resolution is synonymous with sight. You have to make both parties "see" how miniscule the difference is and how easily it can be resolved. Once you have gotten to the root cause of the dispute, you must successfully show both parties that no matter the cause, it is not worth shedding the precious blood of another human being.

CHAPTER 15

YOUTH LEADERSHIP
10 STEPS TO BEING YOUNG AND IN CHARGE

"A DO NOTHING mentality creates a HAVE NOTHING reality". — *@DericMuhammad*

Leadership is a lot like waking up in the morning; the earlier you get started, the more you are likely to get accomplished. Did you know that Dr. Martin Luther King Jr. was only 26 years old when he led the Bus Boycott in Montgomery, Alabama? What you may not know is that he was preparing himself for his mission since he was 15 years old. Too often we look at leaders in our society and are amazed by their accomplishments, but we have no idea how early they started or what they have had to endure.

Nelson Mandela was expelled from a South African college at the age of 22 for participating in a protest. Huey P. Newton was only 23 when he co-founded the legendary Black Panther Party. Tiger Woods appeared on television in a golf putting competition against talk show host Bob Hope when he was only two years old. Venus and Serena Williams started playing tennis so early that they that were able to turn pro at the age of 14. Entertainers like Michael Jackson, Beyonce' Knowles and even Lil' Wayne started working on their craft as children. These individuals are not all considered "leaders" in the traditional sense, but they all lead in their respective fields. The one thing they all have in common is that they didn't become great overnight. True greatness takes time; and the longer it takes for you to get started the longer it will take for you to start shining.

The Bible teaches us that Jesus started His mission at the age of twelve. Since He started so early, who are we to think that we should not?   I am in no way comparing these other people to Jesus. I'm merely highlighting a principle as well as rejecting the mentality that associates being young with "playtime" and leadership to the older generation. You should note that a large majority of revolutionary changes that have taken place around the globe have been spearheaded by young people. Che Guevara and Fidel Castro led the Cuban revolution while in their twenties. Barack Obama's ascendancy as the Democratic nominee of the 2008 presidential election can be taken as a sure sign that it is time for young leadership to take their rightful place in society.

That will never occur as long as a young person's life is solely devoted to partying, girl or boy-chasing, drinking and having a "so-called" good time.

One of the gravest educational crimes committed against young people in America is the absence of courses in leadership and personal finance. Leadership development must become a priority in our communities if we truly want to invest in the future of this country. Here are a few effective leadership tips to consider:

1] VISION is the first element of leadership. You must know where you want to go, what you want to accomplish and who you want to become. The sooner you figure it out the faster you will get there. Too many young people enter college without knowing what discipline they want to master. Living without a vision can be compared to driving blindfolded. You'll end up wherever the vehicle takes you. Life is your vehicle. Take of the blindfolds and get where you are going. A.S.A.P.

2] PURPOSE is the fuel of life. Every person on earth was born with a purpose. True happiness comes from fulfillment of that purpose. The Honorable Elijah Muhammad used to say that purpose can usually be found in that which a person loves to do and that which a person does very well without trying very hard. If you are not afraid to pursue what you love and do it well you will become successful and fulfilled.

3] Set trends, don't follow them! There is entirely too much "imitation and not enough of originality" among the youth of today. Like Russell Simmons says, "DO YOU!" The study of snowflakes reveals there are no two that are the same. You are greater than a snowflake, so stop melting yourself trying to be like someone else. Be yourself, but more importantly be intelligent about it. A successful (You) will inspire others to do the same.

4] START NOW! In Japan, when a mother wants her child to be a mathematician she starts reading Math books aloud to her baby while it is still in her womb. If that is the case, we are all late starters. Regardless, you are never too young to get started on the road to greatness.

5] FIND OPPORTUNITY IN ADVERSITY. If dog poop can fertilize the Earth then anything negative can serve a positive purpose. **Your Attitude toward adversity must be one that seeks to find opportunity in it.** Turn negatives into positives. If your father was not there for you, use that pain as motivation to be a better parent. Or, you can mentor a fatherless child so that they will not experience similar pains. If you can manage to turn your failures into lessons and keep moving towards your goals then you have never really failed.

6] THE "AND-WHAT" FACTOR.   You must be courageous. Too many human beings are absolutely paralyzed by the fear of what others will think of them. You will never become a leader by listening to and following the crowd. Figure out what is right, and then do it. Find out the truth, and then tell it. Be bold about your vision, and then take charge. Work hard until you succeed, and then look back at your critics and say, "and what"!

7] LOVE YOUR HATERS.   You must use the energy of your haters as fuel. If you have no haters you are not working hard enough. When somebody says "you can't do that", even if it is your mother, use it as inspiration to prove them wrong. Most importantly, sometimes a hater will say something against you that is true and give you an opportunity to correct that "something" and be a better person.

Never take it personal. It is a part of this business called leadership.

8] READ or DO NOT LEAD. All great men and women are avid readers. Power is not limited to physical size and strength. There are leaders who rule the world from wheelchairs. They understand mind over matter. In sports it is the huge guys who make the plays on the field and the court, but it is often the puny guys who write the checks. Which would you rather be?

9] NEVER PLAY THE BLAME GAME. Men and women are not creatures of circumstance. Circumstances are creatures of men and women. Anything done can be undone. Anything wrong can be made right. Never blame others when you come up short. Analyze, correct, dust your knees off and get back to work. Leaders do not make excuses. Leaders make progress.

10] EAVESDROP. Find someone who is successful at what you want to do and study them closely. Ask them to mentor you. Work for them for free if you need to. Knowledge is priceless. Study them intensely, but always keep in mind the question "how can I do this better".

Bonus: ALWAYS STRIVE TO BE FIRST! Nobody grows up wanting to be vice president.

It is natural to want to be number one in everything. No one is first in everything, but everyone can be first in something. Start with school grades, athletic competition or community service.

Practice always being number one and get used to it. Go for the gold in whatever you do. If you get the silver, go home and paint it gold, put your shoulder to the plow and get back to work. Think like a leader!

CHAPTER 16

The Secret Relationship: Rappers and Jews

Hip-hop as an art form and a culture is hands down one of the most powerful international social forces in the history of the world. There is not a nation on earth where its footprints cannot be found. Rap artists who create the soundtrack that fuels hip-hop culture become equally influential. They determine trends and the general course of youth culture globally. While it appears these artists who often peddle images of invincibility are in control of hip-hop, we must look deeper to see who may be in control of them.

Rap artist, Jay-Z and once business partner, Damon Dash built a hip-hop powerhouse called Roc-a-fella Records. It was a Black-owned record label that produced millions in sales. As is often the case, these two brothers reportedly had personal and business disagreements and decided to part ways. Legend has it that a Def Jam Records executive by the name of Lyor Cohen played the role of instigator, negotiator and "clean-up" businessman.

What is clear is that Roc-a-Fella Records, once known

as "The Dynasty", is now owned by Def Jam. Cohen happens to be Jewish.

In the late eighties, so-called "gangsta rap" took the nation by storm when a young Black entrepreneur named Eric Wright a.k.a. "Eazy E" assembled some of the finest talent to be found in the Los Angeles/Compton area to form the legendary collective N.W.A. The group captured an untapped market selling millions of albums with no commercial radio play. These record sales did wonders to fill the coffers of Ruthless Records, which was owned by Wright who took on a partner by the name of Jerry Heller. Heller was a veteran music executive who once represented artists like Marvin Gaye. The group's most creative geniuses, Ice Cube and Dr. Dre, eventually left the group citing unfair compensation. Accusations flew that Eazy conspired with Heller to rob the other members of royalties that were rightfully theirs. Heller happens to be Jewish. It should be noted that Ice Cube later made a song threatening Heller. The ADL (Jewish Anti-Defamation League) labeled it anti-Semitic.

Dr. Dre left Ruthless Records and co-founded Death Row Records, a boutique subsidiary of Interscope Records. Death Row's co-founder, Suge Knight, built an impressive roster of talented artists and dominated the charts selling millions of records generating hundreds of millions in revenue. Again, disagreements between the two brothers ended in a parting of ways. Dr. Dre walked away from Death Row Records, who at that time had acquired the legendary Tupac Shakur. After selling millions on Death Row/Interscope, Tupac was murdered. A series of personal and professional misfortunes landed Knight in prison and the house that he and Dre built ended up in the hands Interscope which is owned by a man by the name of Jimmy Iovine. Mr. Iovine happens to be Jewish.

Before this becomes repetitive , let me say that the three aforementioned cases are about as substantive as a teardrop in the Pacific Ocean when compared to the decades of draconian record contracts, usury and the general slave/slavemaster relationship between Black entertainers and music executives who happen to be Jewish. Jewish hegemony in the music world is about as American as apple pie. It has even been said that the second language of the music business is "Yiddish." Truth be told, the Black/Jewish relationship

in the music industry has played a major role in the

rotting of Black/Jewish relationships in general.

Some of our greatest icons, such as Sammy Davis Jr., Billie Holiday, "Little" Richard (and the list goes on) lived rich, yet died broke while Jewish managers, accountants, attorneys, business advisors and others fed their families for years off of their music. Few entertainers in the history of Black America have been able to say that their assets and true net worth were as prominent as their talent and popularity. Sadly, hip-hop is no different. And while hip-hop has produced a handful of millionaires, they are as a teardrop in the Pacific Ocean when compared to the many rappers who, like most Black people, are living "show-to-show" and "check-to-check."

There have been many examples of independent success in hip-hop's music industry such as Master P (No Limit Records), James Prince (Rap-a-Lot Records), Luther Campbell (2 Live Records) and others. However, because none of these outfits had the power to control their own distribution they were eventually left at the mercy of those who did. Who are the owners and controllers of the distribution channels that deliver rap music to the world? You guessed it. They just happen to be Jewish. Cash Money/Young Money Records, a popular imprint from New Orleans who houses artists Lil' Wayne, Drake, Nicki Minaj and others reportedly has one of the last lucrative independent deals in existence, but still do not control their own distribution. Even those Black-owned rap labels who appear to be the front-runners are in a dangerous position.

My critique is not an effort to weaken the powerful image of our great hip-hop artists. I love hip-hop. I am part of the hip-hop generation. This is why I felt the need to write this essay. Hip-hop is leading the youth of the world, but if our artists are under the inordinate control of those who control their careers then where will the youth of the world be led? I'm only trying to, as they say in the streets, "keep it 100." It's time for rappers to become just as tough and assertive in the boardroom as they are in the recording booth.

There is only one solution to this problem: **UNIFY!** Artists need to convene a private meeting of some sorts to determine the best way to chart a course that frees hip-hop artists from such inordinate control. We must learn how to settle differences among ourselves so that our personal disagreements don't leave Black-owned companies, like Roc-a-fella Records, in the hands of the "clean-up men." The enormous influence of a collective group of hip-hop artists backed by the Black community could hold enough weight to make these crooked executives bend to its collective will. The only solution to this problem is UNITY, organization, fearlessness, selflessness and the desire to free the art form and its culture from the control of outside forces. Here is a classic example of what I am suggesting.

In the early 2000s, it was rumored that Irv, along with Death Row Records co-founder Suge Knight and Rap-A-Lot CEO James Prince, was looking to start a black-owned record distribution company. Gotti, however, revealed that the now-aborted plan was much bigger.

"It wasn't a distribution; it was a union. In the music business, the artists, we have no union. There's no health care, it's nothing like that. It should be done," Gotti said, crediting Suge with devising the plan.

"It was all his plan, and it was a hell of a plan," Irv said of the union that would include all artists of every genre. "He was like, 'OK, say you got a million-dollar budget. We're gonna make the record label make it a million and one.' Now, this will all get recouped back to the artist, but that hundred thousand will go for the union."

Under the plan, record labels would front the union dues to artists by including the extra money in their recording budgets. The artist would then have to pay the label back the recoupable costs, just as they would with any advance when their album is sold. In theory, the deal would provide artists with necessary health care and retirement plan options. "Now you can take your kids to [the doctor] — because we have no insurance, no dental, no nothing," he said. "It'll go towards an annuity, it'll go towards a retirement fund, so now when you're a rapper and you aren't making so many records no more, maybe you got a million dollars that built up when you were hot."

Irv told Sway that he, Suge and Prince even went as far as to meet with the same labor organizers who helped set up the player's union for Major League Baseball, but shortly after, things went awry. "Baseball, football, all the other forms of entertainment have a union, they have representatives, they have pensions, they have all this other stuff. So he was talking everything right, it was right," Gotti said. "The Feds came in shortly after we were talking."

In January 2003, <u>Irv's Murder Inc. New York offices were raided</u> by federal instigators, and the producer and his brother Chris were later charged with money laundering and faced up to 20 years in prison. The <u>Gotti brothers beat the charges in 2005</u>, but despite

Irv's claims, there was no documented link to his case and his plans to unionize the music industry.(Reported by Rob Marksman & Sway Calloway)

If hip-hop is to escape the fate of every genre that has come before it, we must pool our resources and combine the genius among us to control our own production, manufacturing, distribution and destiny. Jewish control over artists and entertainers has been the order of the day for much too long. Through the power of right guidance and unity we can break this cycle. But, if we remain disunited, we will pass down to the next generation another cultural force that is under the control of another people.

Last, but not least, artists must follow the footsteps of artists like Chuck D and "fight the power." Never be afraid to challenge those who you know are robbing you of what is rightfully yours. If we don't we are not being true to the root of what we say hip-hop culture represents. Artists should not be afraid to stand up to the outside forces that control hip-hop. On the contrary, artists should be afraid of what will happen if they do not.

CHAPTER 17

Modern Technology: The Gift and The Curse

Every rose has its thorn. The same instrument used to make incisions necessary for surgery can also be used to stab someone to death. While the instrument is neutral, the way it is utilized determines whether it facilitates life or death. So it is with modern technology.

The purpose of technology should be reserved for the advancement of civilization. Technology should help us accomplish life's tasks faster; with less error and greater accuracy. In most cases, it serves its purpose. For instance, when researching a cure for a disease like cancer the internet is a great tool. However, this same tool makes pornographic material more available than ever. At the end of the day, technology will help you do exactly what you want to do. Question is: What are you doing?

Some may answer the above question with a resounding "nothing." I contend that modern technology can even aid you in the accomplishment of "doing nothing." If you wake up with the intention of finding a job or studying for an exam, but instead spend hours on end playing your playstation game or perusing the web, you may very well have enlisted the use of modern technology to help you accomplish "nothing" that day.

My daughter is profoundly gifted at spelling. She won a Nation of Islam local spelling bee. Yet when she sends me text messages, she purposely misspells words; the culture of texting among teens. I admit, texting can be a fast and efficient way to communicate. I use it quite often myself. However, the Honorable Elijah Muhammad so wisely taught us that "too much of anything is no good." He also taught us that writing was one of the "lost arts" of our people.

Too much texting forces the brain to compute information in an abbreviated form. It affects the way we write, think and speak. Now we have what society calls "sexting", where sexually charged text messages and photos are exchanged via text message. It seems that our youth are overlooking the rose of technology and are becoming too anxious to toy with its thorns.

The Gift.-There are billions of cellular phones activated around the world. I have been as far as China without losing the capability of communicating with my family thanks to technology. Social networking sites like Facebook, Instagram and Twitter are great places to find classmates, distant relatives and organize events. As seen recently, these sites have the potential to play a major role in revolutionary mobilization.

Were it not for camera-equipped smart-phones we may have never captured the footage of Oscar Grant's murder by an Oakland officer. Wikileaks founder, Julian Assange, used the internet to leak top-secret cables exposing bizarre communication between sovereign nations. Let's face it, were it not for the brilliant use of cutting-edge modern technology during his 2008 campaign, we may not have elected the first Black president of the United States of America. Modern technology is definitely "the gift."

The Curse-The same smart-phone that we use to communicate has what is termed "memory." In it we store everything from telephone numbers, meeting notes, appointments, etc. But, when we have become too dependent on our phone's memory, what happens to our own?

The same social networking sites that helped organize protests are also havens for sexual predators and rapists. The same camera-phone that captured Oscar Grant's murder is being used to video-record teen-aged girls fighting and tearing one another's clothes off in the process; also to leak sex tapes and private photos of unsuspecting persons.

The same internet that Wikileaks used to expose government secrets is being used to steal the identities of millions of people, robbing them of their earnings. People seldom converse at the gym anymore. Why? Everyone wears iPod earbuds. The same YouTube phenomenon that gave Barack Obama a direct platform to communicate with voters is being used to air gang initiations and lewd, lascivious activity. You get the picture. Modern technology is what you make it. It can be the gift or the curse, depending on how you make use of it.

If we choose not to use technology as a vehicle, it will become a vice. It should be used as a vehicle to facilitate and actualize ideas and concepts. It must also be used as a platform to educate, inform, organize and mobilize the masses of our people. The technology itself is neither positive or negative; it is neutral. It can be employed for positive or negative purposes, depending on who is using it. **The way you use technology is an extension of who you are and how you think. Therefore, self-improvement leads to a more productive use of technology.**

Don't spend so much time on FACEBOOK that you neglect to put your FACE in a BOOK. **There is no technology like the human mind. It's a lot smarter than a smart phone. Invest in your mind.** The returns are limitless. Stop totally depending on gadgets to do your thinking for you. Don't allow yourself to lose sight of the importance of the human bond. Stop texting your grandmother. Get up, go over and visit her. Don't let technology make you lazy.

In the Nation of Islam we are given the lesson of the "Lion in a Cage." The Lion is to use Modern Equipment to help him get out of this cage. I contend that the same modern equipment that can be used to get the Lion out of this cage can be used to keep him in it. You are the Lion. How will you use today's modern technology? It is a question that must be answered in the mirror.

CHAPTER 18

A LEAGUE OF OUR OWN

Are Black Athletes and Executives Qualified?

"The Black man and woman of America have only 2 choices...OWN or be owned."- @DericMuhammad

Lebron James is one of the finest athletes that the Black community has ever produced. He is also a budding businessman who keeps company with the likes of Warren Buffet and Jay-Z. He and other young, gifted and Black ballplayers appear to be looking forward to not only winning dunking contests, but also winning thinking contests. The thinking contest is critical to any athlete's personal, professional and financial future. "After the game" it seems that the vast majority of ball handlers end up broke, directionless and unprepared for life. The 2011 NBA lockout was a potential paradigm shift for embattled Black athletes in American sports.

The dispute between owners, players and the reputed ego-maniacal Commissioner David Stern was a *spectacle of disrespect.* Even Veteran sports journalist, Bryant Gumbel, known for the *safeness* of his opinion, accused the commissioner of acting like a modern day plantation owner. From his critically acclaimed HBO show "Real Sports," Gumbel accused Stern of talking to NBA players like they were his "boys." During negotiations, Stern was documented as having put his finger in the faces of certain players. He reportedly demonstrated unnecessary aggression towards men who were obviously physically superior. To many, Gumbel's statement was like Clarence Thomas wearing an "I AM TRAYVON" t-shirt. Essentially, if Bryant Gumbel could make that observation then it must be high time for change.

What will this change look like for Black NBA players and Black athletes in general? Will it mean more money, benefits and less risk in THEIR league? Should we take a closer look at the term "owner" and why Stern's attitude was the way it was towards players? We all witnessed the fallout when James opted to pursue what he believed was in his own best interest by leaving the Cleveland Cavaliers and joining the Miami Heat. Cleveland spent millions courting him to stay, but the moment he made his decision, their true colors were revealed. Cavs owner, Dan Gilbert derided him as a coward. The very fans who once professed their undying love, threatened him and even burned his jersey in the streets. Since this happened to Lebron, any player who thinks it can't happen to them is two fries short of a "happy meal." In the NBA, you're only as good as your last bucket.

NBA players are paid millions, but NBA owners are worth billions. Chances are if the owners acquiesced to players' legitimate and fair demands, their lifestyles would not suffer any at all. Besides that, anything relinquished in negotiations can be recouped in some other creative way. History bears witness to the truth spoken by the great warrior civil rights activist Fannie Lou Hamer who used to say, "If the White man gives you anything—just remember when he gets ready, he'll take it right back."

Sometimes when negotiations break down between two parties it is because the issue is no longer about fairness or truth. It is rather about power and control. Clearly, the NBA owners believe they own not only the teams, but also the human beings who make up the team. In the end, Mr. Gumbel was right. Human beings who think they own other human beings usually reside on plantations. There is only one real solution to this problem.

I believe Black NBA players and executives should pool their resources and start their own league. A slave mentality will deem it an impossible task.

However, the free thinking human being who has studied history only sees it as a *return to independent thinking*.

Our children should be familiar with iconic figures in

Black history like Rube Foster. While it is perfectly fine to acknowledge the accomplishments of Steve Jobs, it is just as acceptable to recognize Black men who have achieved what is now considered impossible. Mr. Foster was a phenomenal pitcher who became the owner of his own team. Also, he was the president of the first successful Negro League – a thriving baseball association that created opportunities for Black talent when Whites would not allow them to play in the "major" leagues. Black people supported the league in droves. The "swagger" of Black athletes outstripped their counterparts with such class that even Whites became fans. The Negro Leagues became a competitive entity. The idea of integration proved to be the undoing of Negro League baseball with Black-owned teams. Today, you are hard pressed to find Black players in pro baseball; and they no longer have the alternative of a league of their own. It is recorded that Rube Foster suffered a mental breakdown and mysteriously died in an insane asylum. He probably went crazy envisioning the future. He probably had nightmares of David Stern pointing his finger in the face of a Black athlete twice his size.

If it was done then with far less resources and technology, it can be done now. But who would have the courage, vision and testicular fortitude to make such a bold and independent move?

If Black athletes decided to "do for self" and start their own league, where would it leave the NBA? The NBA without Black players would be like a bicycle without a chain; going absolutely nowhere. Ticket sales would plummet right along with fan interest. We undoubtedly have the athletic talent to support a league of our own. When combined with the intellectual prowess of Magic Johnson, Michael Jordan, Bob Johnson and others, we have the ability to complete this unprecedented task. When the Honorable Elijah Muhammad asked if Black people in America were qualified to have a nation of our own, he answered an emphatic "yes" to his own question. I humbly submit that if we are qualified to build our own nation, then we must be qualified to start our own sports organizations.

NBA players and executives should wise up. As long as they are the owners and we are just players, they will see us no differently than plantation owners saw sharecroppers. The players may be well paid, but they fail to understand that the more they pay you, the more of you they think they own.

Once an agreement has been made, you still have no choice except to return to their houses (NBA teams), because you have failed to see the writing on the wall. Once you have returned to their houses, they will craftily find a way to make you play by their rules. White people have been making and breaking treaties for a long, long time.

It is a good thing to see players unite and stand for their own enlightened self-interest in 2011. But I say they should have taken a page from Rube Foster's life and started A LEAUGE OF OUR OWN.

CHAPTER 19

THE HOODIE EXPERIMENT

If Jesus came back to save the world how would He be received if He chose to show up in a hoodie? If the "cover of darkness" that He decided to come under were a Black fleece hooded sweatshirt, and He arbitrarily walked in and sat on the back row of the church, synagogue or the mosque, how would we respond? These are questions that swim around in my head every winter when I pull my hoodies out and decide that I don't want my bald head to freeze over. There is something about a young, Black male in a hoodie that makes everyone want to double check to make sure their doors are locked. When, in reality, some of us are just trying to keep our ears warm.

As a member of the Nation of Islam, I was trained to wear a suit practically every day. The Honorable Elijah Muhammad dresses his followers in business attire, because he wanted to prepare us to meet with the business people of the entire world. He also taught us that "opposites attract"; that we should not go among our people offering what we have been taught looking exactly as they do. These are profound lessons that every Black man in America can benefit from.

When I am "dressed up" in a custom suit, I am usually treated with some form of distinction. White people can't help but at some point ask, "excuse me, sir, you look so sharp and well-spoken, what do you do?" That's their way of saying with political correctness, "you don't look like the rest of the nigg**s." If I am recognized for my activist role in the community, I am sometimes treated with some form of honor. However, when I am "dressed down" in my jeans, sneakers and my "hoodie," I get the opportunity to see how young Black males are treated for real. People double-lock their doors, clutch their pocketbooks, decide to wait for "the next elevator" and can be generally rude. It's a more profound experience when you change from your three-piece suit to your hoodie on the same day. It's as if the world becomes a different place. While I recognize the power of presentation and how wearing a suit and tie can afford you some visible advantages, I also recognize that not every brother has a suit or tie and I am more concerned about the way my people are treated "dressed down" than the way I am treated "dressed up."

Some of you are thinking this treatment is justified, because these youngsters *just need to pull up their pants.* I agree, in part. Walking around with your boxer stains on display is not the way to earn respect.

We feel this way because the Black male image has been hijacked, repackaged and demonized by the mass media.

When we see a Black male wearing a hoodie, we automatically think of "O-Dog" (from the movie Menace to Society) shooting the owner of a convenience store because he said something about his mother. We don't look at the man in the hoodie and think "Wow, I wonder if that's Brother Deric under there." The reality is that it just might be.

A more important reality is that the biggest thieves, murderers and robbers in the country wear suits; not hoodies. You should be even more afraid when you see them coming.

As a young student of revolution, I studied the life of the late great Libyan leader Col. Maummar Ghadafi. An unforgettable story is told about his early days as the leader of the country when he was about 28 or 29 years of age. He used to slip away from his security, dress up in disguise and disappear into the streets among the homeless, destitute, poor and hopeless people of Libya. As the president and leader of a nation, he would live on the streets for weeks at time. He was trying to better connect himself to their experience so that he could make effective decisions for them. This afforded him the opportunity to see firsthand what their needs were. It better equipped him to be able to serve them, despite the negative press he received. Ghadafi was willing to put himself in the shoes of the least, the last and the lost in order to see what his people were suffering at the moment. I found this to be a very powerful tool.

There are various ways for leadership to do this. Pastors and ministers should go to great length to find out how common people are treated when they enter the doors of their churches. A church, mosque or synagogue who treats the least member the same way the pastor or minister is treated is one that God would be pleased with. Leaders should call anonymously to their own organizations and get a feel for how common, everyday people are treated.

News reporters should go and anonymously stand in a line to recieve government assistance and see how mothers who may have hit a tough time in life are treated. What a story that would make! We live in a society that doesn't give a damn about how common people are treated, because people in leadership are too busy worried about how they, themselves are treated. It is the culture of a society that was built on slave labor. I am not simply speaking about the way Whites treat Blacks. I am speaking about the way we treat one another.

If you have lost your compassion for the way everyday people are treated, then your leadership will be short-lived. God is turning the page as we speak.

Jesus set the standard for nearness to Him by saying that the mistreatment of "the least of these, My brethren" represented the mistreatment and neglect of Jesus Himself, (Matthew 25:40). Go and read it for yourself. Leadership is only as good as the treatment afforded to the least of those that they are supposed to be serving.

If every Black male in a hoodie were unintelligent then Jay-Z would not be a multi-millionaire. If every man in a suit were to be trusted then Bernie Madoff would not have become a multi-billionaire scheming hard-working families out of millions of dollars. More crimes are committed in Brooks Brothers suits than in Roc-a-wear hoodies.

Be careful not to base your opinions of others on the images you see on TV. Jesus might just decide to make His return wearing a hoodie just to see how we treat "the least of our brethren." I encourage all professionals, preachers, parents, politicians, leaders and others to take the "Hoodie Experiment."

Just put on a hoodie one day and get a glimpse of how our young people are treated. If you choose not to do that, just find a way to put yourself directly in the shoes of the people you are supposed to serve. When you see how they are treated it may give you some insight into why they act the way they act. Most of you think you know their experience, but you really don't. **No individual can rise above the condition of his or her people**. So even, if you wear a suit most days like me, or President Obama, at some point society will remind you of this.

Our president is a well-dressed world leader, but considering the way he is treated by a certain demographic in America, he may as well wear a hoodie every day.

Learn to look beneath the hoodie and beyond the cuff links. If we are unwilling to look beyond the surface we will never be able to find the substance. And we need the substance in order to survive.

CHAPTER 20

ELDER EXPLOITATION

The Culture of Ungratefulness

Ms. Mary is one of the sweetest elderly ladies you could ever meet. She has lived in her fragile home in the Houston Heights neighborhood for over 50 years. She never leaves her humble abode without her black suitcase, which she proudly rolls on its squeaky wheels. She takes it to the grocery store, post office and everywhere. Most of the young jet-setters in her neighborhood think she is strange.

To the contrary, Ms. Mary is wise. She is so smart that she has held on to her land to the chagrin of developers who have built swanky $300,000 three-story condos around her. She knows that her balcony, despite its rotting wood, provides the Heights' most beautiful view of the downtown Houston skyline. It is a view that holds many memories for her, but means millions of dollars to those developers.

Ms. Mary says that she's been harassed for at least a decade about her property. Lawyers, realtors and builders have tried to buy her property at less than half its true value. She says they've vandalized her home and done "all kinds of ugly things" to strike enough fear in her to sell low so they can profit big. The black suitcase that she carries is filled with important paperwork; tax receipts, property deeds and court documents that prove that she is the sole owner of her properties. She fears that if she leaves her documents at home, "they" will break into her home again and steal the only proof that she has that her property belongs to her.

If you think that Ms. Mary is overreacting, you should travel across town to southeast Houston to visit Ms. Johnson. She is the elderly lady who earlier this summer sent her son to landscape one of the many lots she owns in Sunnyside and got a huge surprise. Her son returned and told her he could not cut the grass. When asked why, he calmly revealed that someone had illegally built a brand new home on the property and there was a "for sale" sign in the yard.

Ms. Johnson hired an attorney who investigated the matter and discovered fake and forged documents indicating Ms. Johnson's sale of the property.

These are two among the increasingly frequent calls that I have been receiving about elder abuse and the manipulation of senior citizens in our community. It is an issue that is commanding more and more attention, as our grandmothers, grandfathers, great aunts and uncles become the prey of unscrupulous individuals, contractors and corporations looking to turn a profit at their expense.

Certain cultures emphasize the honor, respect and dignity of the elderly. Many countries count it a badge of honor to have grown old. There are no such things as "old folk homes". There is no such thing as an argument over who is going to take care of grandma when grandma can no longer care for herself. It's simple. The same people that she took care of her entire life should be overjoyed to care for her in the twilight of her life.

There is a saying that my uncle used to repeat; "once an adult, twice a child." Not to sound insensitive to the plight of the elderly, but if you are blessed to reach old age, chances are you won't be able to take care of yourself as you did when you were younger. The cycle of life dictates that everything that is blessed to live gets old. Guess what? That means you and me, too. If you want to know what its like to get old…just keep living. God forbid when we are at the age of fragility we are left to be taken advantage of by the pariahs of society who feed on the elderly.

We must develop a new attitude about our elders in the Black community. We are standing on their shoulders and benefiting from their sacrifice and struggle every day. We must sit, listen to, write down and record the extensive wisdom from their years of life experience. We cannot afford to bury their wisdom along with their bodies when they make their physical transitions. We must teach our children the importance of and respect for their elders. Failure to do so may very well secure our own seat in the old folks home.

I believe there should be harsher laws put in place for those who exploit and abuse the elderly for personal profit. While there a many great facilities that house and care for the elderly, there are just as many that treat them as burdens rather than the jewels of society. There should be a task force put in place to closely monitor them all so that not one elder is abused by some lunatic posing as a caretaker.

If you have a family member who is elderly you should call and check on them today. If you know of an elderly person in the community who does not have anyone, you should adopt him or her by checking on them periodically, but consistently. You have no idea how your presence will lift their spirits.

And if they try to talk you to death…just sit there and listen.

I would like to give a special thanks to the SHAPE Community Center and all other organizations and groups that have created consistent programs for the elders. **Without them, there would be no us.**

CHAPTER 21

NO INDIVIDUAL CAN RISE ABOVE THE CONDITION OF HIS PEOPLE

One Saturday morning I attended a workshop where my younger brother and Journalist Jesse Muhammad, was a featured presenter. Afterward, I decided to take a shopping stroll through the Galleria Mall to exchange some merchandise. I parked near the Neiman Marcus entrance and was exiting to return to my car, bags in hand, when I noticed an upper middle-aged White female getting out of her Cadillac.

As she proceeded towards the mall entrance, the first person she saw was me. I was a clean-cut fellow wearing a custom-made business suit and tie with both hands full of shopping bags. I had a white hanky in my pocket, and donned spit-shined Italian shoes, cuff links and all. But when she clutched her purse and ignored my "how you doing", I realized that all she saw was just another ni---r walking by.

It's not like I've never experienced this before. Growing up as a Black male in America I've had many purses "clutched" as I walked by. I thought that maybe it had something to do with the way I was dressed as a youth or the hole in my t-shirt because I grew up poor. However, while a lot has changed in my life, one thing hasn't. I am still a Black man in America and whether I wear a Hugo Boss suit or sagging blue jeans I am still subject to the "old purse clutch."

Remember when Harvard professor Henry Louis "Skip" Gates was arrested by the Cambridge Police Department for "being upset" in his own home he fell under the same law. Professor Gates is too intelligent to believe that what happened to him does not happen to Black males every minute in America. He knows that racial profiling is a pandemic. He just did not imagine it happening to him after all the university hours he's put in to become an internationally renowned scholar, educator and historian.

On that day the professor became a student again. He became a student of a phrase coined by the Honorable Elijah Muhammad that should be adopted as a law. It says that "no one individual can ever rise above the condition of his or her people." Brothers in the hood were like welcome to the real world Professor Gates.

Professor Gates made the mistake of thinking that a certain social status, level of education, wealth and influence should have separated him from the discrimination that his people received daily. Although the hallways of his home were reportedly littered with photos of the professor taken with presidents, dignitaries and others, that police officer saw him the same as the old White lady in the Cadillac saw me that day; just another ni---r.

President Barack Obama fell under the same law during a visit to Russia. While greeting Russian dignitaries alongside Russia's president, he noticed that the dignitaries would shake everyone else's hand but his. They refused to shake Obama's hand. Even though he is the President of the United States of America, they saw him just like that old White lady in the Cadillac saw me.

There goes that law again. How much higher can one rise in this world's society except to become the President of the United States? And if Obama can't get around this law then any Black man or woman in America who thinks they can is a fool.

Not even the late-great Michael Jackson could escape the law. Once he was no longer under "their control" they crucified him in the media, hurled false charges at him, made him undergo physical strip searches and treated him the same way they'd treat a petty drug dealer on a corner in Brooklyn.

Jesus' disciples were confused about certain statements He made to them. For all intents and purposes they felt like they'd treated the Master well. But Jesus made it clear when He said, "Inasmuch as you have not done this to the least of these(My people), you have also not done it unto Me." Jesus was saying that true progress can only be measured by what we do for the least of God's people. **When the least of our people rise, we all rise.**

While individual success can and should be applauded; always remember that no one individual can ever rise above the condition of his or her people.

Bonus Chapter

THE SECRET TO ATTRACTING A REAL MAN:
(Interview with H2H Magazine)

H2H: Generally speaking and then personally speaking, what is your view of beauty as it relates to a woman? How do you see that regarding the Law of Attraction? What are some misconceptions women may have as it relates to what they think men believe beauty is?

Deric Muhammad (DM): When you talk about beauty as it relates to the female and the view of a man, there is a saying that "beauty is in the eye of the beholder." It suggests that what is beautiful to one man may not be beautiful to the next. In a great way beauty has a lot to do with how a person thinks, and how a person thinks is influenced by his environment and the society that he grew up in. The way a person thinks is influenced greatly by his motives and his agenda. There are so many different things that motivate the view and vision of a man as it relates to beauty.

One of the things that come to mind in the concept of beauty, where women are concerned; it is greatly influenced by a man's mother. A man who has a good relationship with his mother, which most males do, he sees in his mother great qualities that he stores in his mind. When he goes out to look for a mate he generally chooses a woman that in some way, form or fashion reflects his mother. I've found this to be very, very true.

Another thing that comes to mind is a man's motive. Men are very goal-oriented. If a man is a surface dweller and he's thinking from the point of view of conquering the flesh, then of course his view of beauty will be based on that. A woman who he may consider has a pretty face, an hour glass shape then of course that will get his attention. Why? Because his motive is conquering the flesh and satisfying the flesh. It's a low motive, not necessarily a high motive. You can't attract a man with the attracting power of physical beauty. You can get him, but the question is can you keep him?

In civilized nations men are taught to look deeper than the surface. In most cases when a man pursues a woman he's trying to figure out whether or not this woman would be the person he could spend the rest of his life with. A pretty face just won't get it. An hour glass shape just won't get it. That comes a dime a dozen. However, when a man is looking for a woman he is going to spend the rest of his life with and who can possibly be the mother of his children, the qualities he looks for are internal and not necessarily external.

Don't get me wrong, every man who is a natural man will be attracted to the physical beauty of a woman. However, once you get past the physical beauty and the attitude is bad and the vanity is there and the arrogance is there, all of that begins to override the physical beauty. Trust me, a pretty woman with a bad attitude can turn ugly very fast. At some point, the man will want to move around to see what else is out there, because at the end of the day real beauty is not external, it's internal. Therefore, good men look for women who have external beauty, but he wants that external beauty to be a reflection of internal beauty. Not a woman who has external but internally ugly. That's just not beautiful at all.

The Law of Attraction says that you attract what you are. In other words, you attract what you think. As a man thinketh so is he. In the Western world, we've been taught, either directly or indirectly, that the standard of beauty is and always has been the white woman. That affects the way that we think. So for years the dark-skinned sisters whose African features were more prominent then the European features of the slave master, wore her hair natural versus pressing it and perming it. She struggled with herself and the way she was viewed by Black men in America, in Europe and in the West in general. That is now changing, because as the old world goes out and the New World comes in, that which is Original becomes more popular. Now you see more sisters wearing their hair natural. At one point, having full lips was said to be something that was bad, and now folks are getting lip injections and tanning the skin; that's a multi-billion dollar business. So it went from us trying to be like them, to them trying to be like us, and when I say "us" I'm saying the Original people. It just goes to show that beauty is in the eye of the beholder, because what was considered beautiful 30 years ago is not necessarily considered beautiful today.

What we see on the outside, often, is just a reflection of the society in which we live and the way that it coaches us to think. We have to begin looking internally to recognize the beauty on the inside. When you find a woman who is beautiful on the inside and the beauty on the outside is just a reflection of what's on the inside that is a woman that a man can truly love.

I think that women make the mistake of thinking that external beauty is enough to get them through when it's not. You have to work on yourself from the inside out; not from the outside in.

H2H: Yes sir, so all of those colored contact lenses, weaves, et cetera don't really hold much weight as much as a woman would think in terms of attracting a man and keeping his attention.

DM: We're taught in the Nation of Islam about the scientific process by which the Caucasian was made and the scientists who were responsible for the grafting of the Original man into what we see now as the Caucasian. We're taught by the Honorable Elijah Muhammad that he (Yakub) did it through a concept called attracting power. It says that opposites attract and that which is alike repels. There is scientific power in the law of attraction. Therefore, a sister can dress herself up in a certain way where she can achieve attractiveness. When you've dressed yourself up in an attractive way and you walk around the mall and it's clearly visible that everybody's looking at you, the question you must ask yourself is "what am I attracting"?

There are different levels of attracting power. When a sister decides she will go outside disrobed, revealing certain body parts that should only be reserved for a man who has decided to take the responsibility of being her husband, she may attract the kind of man that she doesn't want in her life long term, number one. Number two, and I'm just going to be real and honest, a man does not respect a woman who is disrobed as much as he respects a woman who is robed or a woman who dresses modestly. Men have a higher respect and a higher regard for women who dress modestly than they do for women who don't. We should respect all women and respect all sisters, but when you put what they call your "T & A" on display and you expect a man to respect you for your mind, then unfortunately you attract men that are not looking at you for the beauty of your mind or the majesty of your intelligence. You're attracting those who are looking at you for what you have on display.

When you walk by the department store there's a display. There's a dummy in the window. The merchandise is on the dummy. The person who's shopping enters into the store, because something in the window has attracted them to come on in. The question I ask my sisters is what is it you have on display? Don't be like the dummy in the window thinking that you can display a certain thing that would attract a man to come into that store, but then be angry at him once he gets into the store and he's pretty much looking for what you had on display. He ain't looking for anything else except what you had on display.

H2H: You just reminded me of many situations that I find myself in when I have on my garment, and I attend these different galas or networking events where everyone is dressed in suits or less. When I come in my Muslim garment, the attention that that particular garment receives probably takes a lot of the attention away from a woman who is less dressed. When you say that the mind of that man is a factor or key component in terms of what he's attracted to or what catches his eye, I've seen that firsthand by being covered up, beautifully, but covered. The level of respect was certainly apparent. Those brothers were breaking their necks just to open the door for me. I definitely see the difference just from those experiences.

DM: A woman who covers herself is beautiful to all men. What the woman who does not cover herself fails to understand is that the woman who covers herself and covers herself beautifully – she's not walking around with a blanket on – she has attracting power as well; a different type of attracting power. When she walks into a room where so many sisters are half dressed, she becomes the opposite that attracts.

Now, the sister who has on very little clothes and the sister who is in her garment looking beautiful, they both attract attention and they both will attract some attention that is positive and some they would be negative. There are pros and cons. The sister in the "Daisy Duke" shorts thinks that getting any kind of attention is a plus to her, but at the same time the sister is also a prime target for a rapist, she's a prime target for a molester and she's a prime target for a woman to be disrespected.

The sister who wears a modest garment gets all kind of positive feedback from men and women, but particularly from men. However, she can also get some kind of negative feedback. Let's say she's a

Muslim and she's covered in her Muslim garment. Her garment identifies her as a follower of Prophet Muhammad (PBUH) or a follower of the Honorable Elijah Muhammad. Because these are hated men by the Western world her garment could attract some form of negative attention, but because she has covered herself and she's striving to be righteous, God always protects the righteous sister. Therefore, the negative attention that the sister in her garment gets earns the protection of God even when there's negative attention. However, the sister who is not covered puts herself in position where she takes herself out from underneath that divine protection and it works against her. At the end of the day, for the sister who covers herself; her positives always outweigh her negatives as far as attention is concerned. Yet, the sister who does not cover herself, her negatives always outweighs her positives. That's for the sister out there who knows, in her heart, that she should be covered. She's a Christian woman, she has read the Bible and she reads where it is prescribed for her that she should cover her bosom and that she should lower the hem of her garment, but she is afraid that she won't get the attention that she once got when she wore clothes that accentuated certain body parts that she believes that men want to see. At the end of the day, those negatives outweigh those positives. Therefore, I urge all of my sisters to lower the hem of their garment.

H2H: Thank you beloved!

DM: Thank you. I like the questions that you asked, because all too often the sisters are fooled. The beauty of a Black woman could fool you. At the end of the day it's an illusion. Minister Farrakhan said it like this, "You can gain a man through the beauty of your form, but you can't keep him like that". You can't keep him with the beauty of your form, because someone will always come along with a form more beautiful. As time goes by gravity works on everything. So what was once a Coke bottle shape one year can overnight turn into a 2-liter (laughing). You just never know what will happen.

H2H: …a milk jug (laughing).

DM: (laughing) She'll turn into a 2-liter on you. You want to make sure that you've chosen a man who whether or not you have a Coke bottle or a 2-liter will love you for what's on the inside and not for what is on the outside.

H2H: Yes sir, and not only gravity and someone more attractive coming along, but you have instances where women go through health issues. She may get into an accident and her face is scarred up, or she loses a limb. She may go through Chemotherapy and lose her hair. There was a case where one woman was burned beyond recognition. Those are some of the things I think about as well, things you can't control.

DM: Right. We live in a society that exalts the flesh and it minimizes the importance of the spirit. What we have to do is minimize the importance of the flesh and exalt that which is spiritual and mental. When we begin to think like that we'll probably make better choices in our mates.

H2H: One more point. Sister Ava (Muhammad) mentioned this on one of her shows a while ago. There was a song by Ludacris, and it was something to the effect of a woman doesn't have to be attractive for him to have sex with her; he'll just get drunk and do it anyway. She was making a point that today we don't even function from physical attractiveness, but now we're functioning off of impulse. I thought that was a heavy point and observation in how this world has taken a turn for the worse. So when you say that the society that we live in now exalts the flesh it now goes beyond being physically attracted to someone, because you can intoxicate yourself and go through with it. You don't care anymore.

DM: Well what Ludacris was saying was that he just wanted to satisfy the flesh, and because a woman that he deemed to be attractive wasn't available, he said, "Well you know what, I'll just take what I got sitting right here in front of me and what I'll do is inebriate myself. If I inebriate myself then just maybe I can give myself an excuse in the morning for sleeping with this person".

That's what lets you know, number one, that it's all an illusion and number two, in reinforces the idea that women can only be used for tools of pleasure. However, it's like the Minister says, "It's difficult for a woman who does not respect herself to demand respect". Even with a brother like Ludacris, he's looking for that right sister that he can marry. Every man is looking for that in some way, form or fashion. I believe every man is looking for that right woman.

We can critique Ludacris for saying something like that, and we should because that's not right, but we have to also ask ourselves the question – the sister that he's talking about – how did she present herself to him? It's like when you go on a job interview you present yourself in a way that fosters the perception of how you wish to be viewed. Therefore, my question to my sisters is, how do you want to be perceived? Based upon the way you want to be perceived, you should present yourself in a way that fosters that perception.

H2H: Beautifully said. Thank you very much for your thoughts beloved.

DM: Thank you, I appreciate the opportunity.

ABOUT THE AUTHOR

Deric Muhammad is a Houston-based community activist.
For more info he can be reached at
www.dericmuhammad.com